Proven Leadership Strategies

A Novel for Navigating Storms

Harold Gallaher

Peter Schrock

Copyright © 2025 by Peter Schrock and Harold Gallaher

Appendix copyright © 2025 by Harold Gallaher used by permission

All rights reserved.

No portion of this book may be reproduced in any form without permission from the publisher, except as permitted by U.S. copyright law.

For permissions contact: Finest Studios - FinestStudios.net

This novel is a work of fiction. Names, characters, places, and incidents are the product of the author's imagination or are used fictitiously. Any resemblance to actual events, locales, or persons, living or dead, is entirely coincidental.

Publisher's Cataloging-in-Publication Data

Names: Schrock, Peter, author. | Gallaher, Harold, author.

Title: Proven Leadership Strategies: A Novel for Navigating Storms / by Peter Schrock and Harold Gallaher.

Description: Farmington, MO : Finest Studios, 2025.

ISBN: 979-8-9918052-1-6

Subjects: LCSH: Leadership--Fiction. | Business--Fiction. | Mentoring--Fiction.

Printed in the United States of America

First Edition: August 2025

DEDICATION

To all the people in our lives that have taught us to cherish those around us and have helped us reach our potential.

TABLE OF CONTENTS

Introduction 11
Chapter 1: The Weight of the World 15
Chapter 2: A Man Without a Principle 19
Chapter 3: The Untuned Machine 23
Chapter 4: The Power of a Question 28
Chapter 5: The Hasty Rush 32
Chapter 6: The Leaves or The Tree 37
Chapter 7: The Story of the Cup Dispenser 42
Chapter 8: The Shaken Sack 47
Chapter 9: The Threads of Trust 52
Chapter 10: The Unread Sign 57
Chapter 11: The Golden Silence 61
Chapter 12: The Quickest Payment 66

Chapter 13: The Hidden Streams of Wealth. 70

Chapter 14: The Extra Casting. 75

Chapter 15: The Crucible of Command. 79

Chapter 16: Growing Like Flowers 84

Chapter 17: A Project Without a Champion. 89

Chapter 18: The Other Man's Game 93

Chapter 19: The Drama of the Glasses. 97

Chapter 20: The Anchor at Home 101

Chapter 21: The Final Presentation. 105

Chapter 22: The Anchor Holds 109

Chapter 23: A Sinner in an Old Farm Truck. 112

Chapter 24: Pass It On 117

Chapter 25: Home. 121

Appendix: Harold's "Thin Book". 124

Free Audiobook Download 147

FREE AUDIOBOOK

Download this book as an audiobook for free with your purchase of this print edition by going to the last page in this book.

INTRODUCTION

What is this Book?

Our family was driving when we passed a sign on the side of the road. It was by a large field, and it said something about a public hearing. My wife turned to me and said, "Do you know what that is about?" The field was large and beautifully green with mature trees sprawled across it. It was nestled just outside our city and was prime real estate for anyone hoping to expand the city limits.

"I don't know, but I know someone who would." I was thinking of Harold Gallaher, our County Commissioner, and we would be seeing him shortly. We drove through the rolling hills on our way to church and eventually parked next to a pond with water spraying from a fountain in the center. The Missouri heat was intense as we stepped outside, with humidity that felt like we were breathing water. As we made our way among the streams of people heading for the air-conditioned building, we saw many smiling and greeting faces.

Our church was celebrating its twentieth year since it had started with a handful of people, but now it was a sea. We walked down the corridor, dropping our children off with friends serving in the Sunday school classes. Then I saw him sitting in a chair in the lobby among a few others. His white hair spoke of all the many things he had seen and experienced in life. Someone laughed as they spoke with him. Harold had a serious tone about him, but his witty comments were far from serious. The edge of his lip curled into a smile as everyone broke into laughter this time.

I dropped off one of my daughters at the pre-K room and then made my way back to Harold. He wasn't talking to anyone now, and there was a chair next to him. I sat down on the hard cushion and leaned forward through the noise of the lobby.

"Harold," I started, and he looked at me, raising his eyebrows, "Do you know what the sign out by Bray Road is all about? Are they going to build something?" He paused, his mind searching a vast mental catalog before landing on the right file.

He turned back to me and said, "I think they are considering building a new shopping center there." Now that I had broken the ice, I formulated my real reason for wanting to connect with Harold. Years ago, we had been in a small group together, and I found his experience and history fascinating. He had managed crews, owned businesses, invented things, and was now basically running our county. I am sure there was much more in there, too, but I was impressed by scratching the surface. I had recently taken on a new executive director role, and I was curious if he had any advice for me from within that vast storehouse.

"Harold, do you have any advice for me in my new executive director role?" I asked, looking keenly into his eyes. He paused again for a moment, considering the weight of my question, and shared a few nuggets.

What is this Book?

Then he said, "Actually, I have a 'Thin Book' of lessons I have learned myself and from others that I have recorded. I could give you a copy if you are interested?" I smiled; this was exactly what I wanted. I had been poring through hundreds of books seeking wisdom in the last few years, searching for answers to the questions I had struggled to reconcile. However, many books required me to boil down their contents to pull out their nuggets of insight, and it sounded like Harold's 'Thin Book' would already have done a lot of the hard work.

"I would love to get a copy," I responded, not knowing when or how he would get it to me.

I didn't have to wait long. The next day, as I sat in my office at work, one of my staff stopped in my office with a large manila envelope. I opened it to find a treasure trove of proverbs and stories Harold had compiled. As I read the wisdom, an idea formed in my mind. What if we could help people better remember and relate to all of Harold's insights by compiling them into a master story? Some of my favorite books are allegorical stories that illustrate and teach wisdom. Years earlier, I had written several short stories like this, and I always wanted to write a full novel.

About a week later, my family went on vacation, traveling to visit family and friends in Michigan. On the trip, I cracked open my computer and started to craft a story arc, characters, and incorporated Harold's wisdom. With the advent of A.I., I was able to take the block of wood that contained my ideas and make the initial rough cuts to accelerate each part of the story process that I had learned from companies like Muse and authors on Masterclass. I didn't finish it on the trip, but after several early mornings and evenings crafting and writing, I had a rough draft that I presented to Harold.

Harold loved it and read through it several times. After getting his approval and feedback, I began carving by hand to fix the problems in the plot and intricately developing the details in the characters. I interconnected several parts to loop the story back on itself and carefully found many more ways to integrate Harold's wisdom all over the book. Now, I am excited to share what I have learned from Harold in this engaging format.

At the end of this story, I have included Harold's "Thin Book", so you can see what inspired this adventure and see if you missed any of his insights along the way.

Let the journey begin,

Peter Schrock

CHAPTER 1

The Weight of the World

The object on his desk was a small, wooden chess piece, carved from a single piece of pale-colored, dense wood. It was a pawn, no bigger than his thumb, with a perfectly rounded head on a solid, tiered base. It hadn't been there when he'd collapsed into his chair after the morning's disastrous all-hands meeting. He was sure of it. Mark Trenton picked it up. It felt impossibly heavy for its size, smooth and cool against his skin, a solid, tangible thing in a world that felt like it was dissolving into smoke.

He had no idea who could have left it. His office door was always open—an invitation for interruptions he could no longer afford.

The hum of the servers from the back room was the only sound that answered his unspoken question. It was the sound of money burning.

"This isn't a discussion, people, it's a post-mortem!" his boss, Richard, had thundered earlier, his face the color of a ripe plum. The leadership team had gathered in the main conference room, the air thick with the smell of stale coffee and fear. "Project Chimera is sinking, and it's taking this company down with it. I want answers. Not excuses. Answers!"

Mark had felt a dozen pairs of eyes slide toward him. As Operations Manager, Chimera was his baby. A monstrous, malformed, and very, very sick baby.

"The core issue seems to be a cascade failure in the supply chain," Mark had started, his voice sounding thin even to his own ears.

"Seems to be?" David, the head of marketing, had pounced on the words, his smile a predatory slash. "Seems to be, Mark? We're six weeks past our launch date, bleeding market share to a competitor that didn't even exist a year ago, and we're still operating on what it seems to be?"

David was a master of the vague accusation, the kind of corporate assassin who could kill you with a well-placed question mark. He spoke of brand synergy and market penetration, but Mark had never once seen him produce a spreadsheet that contained a real number. It was all feeling, all gut, all expensive, flashy nonsense.

"What's your proposal, David?" Richard had asked, turning up the heat.

"We need to be aggressive. A full-spectrum marketing blitz. Re-contextualize the narrative. We're not late; we're perfecting. We're not failing; we're innovating."

Mark had wanted to scream. Innovating what? A new form of bankruptcy? But he'd held his tongue. The problem wasn't the narrative; it was the product. And the product was failing because the parts were failing. But he didn't have the data to prove it, not yet. He just had the worry—a cold, heavy knot in his stomach that had been his constant companion for months. It was a corrosive feeling, a worry that didn't lead to solutions, only to sleepless nights and a paralyzing sense of dread.

Now, hours later, the office was a ghost town. 7:17 PM. The glow of his monitor painted a map of failure across his face. The sales dashboard was a waterfall of red arrows. He clicked it away, revealing the spreadsheet beneath—a meaningless jumble of figures that blurred into an indictment of his leadership.

His phone buzzed on the desk, a sharp, angry sound in the silence. A text from his wife, Jen.

Colton's team won. He scored a goal. He kept looking for you in the stands.

The words hit him like a physical blow, knocking the wind out of him. He squeezed his eyes shut, the image of his son's hopeful face turning to disappointment searing itself into his mind. He saw the drawing Colton had left on his pillow that morning—a stick-figure family, all holding hands, except for one figure, noticeably detached, holding a briefcase.

The weight of it all—the failing project, the condescending peer, the disappointed son—pressed down on him. He felt like a man trying to build a fortress on quicksand. He was losing at work. He was losing at home.

He opened his eyes, and his gaze fell on the small, wooden pawn still clutched in his hand. It was a stark contrast to the digital chaos on his screen and the emotional chaos in his heart. It was simple. Solid. Real.

Where had it come from?

He turned it over and over, his thumb tracing the smooth lines of its base. As he set it down, he noticed a tiny, folded piece of paper tucked beneath where it had been. He unfolded it. On it were a few words written in a precise, elegant script: Oak Park. Pond. 8 PM. The silent, enigmatic object now had an instruction. It felt like a question, a mystery dropped into the middle of his collapsing world. For the first time all day, a feeling other than anxiety flickered within him: a spark of pure, undiluted curiosity. He had no way of knowing it then, but the answer to who had left the pawn was far less important than the journey it was about to begin.

CHAPTER 2

A Man Without a Principle

Mark slipped the wooden pawn and the mysterious note into his coat pocket. Their combined presence was a tangible weight against his hip on his way out of the quiet office building. As he passed the main corridor, he saw the janitor, Jack, methodically buffing the already gleaming floors. Jack was a fixture in the building, a man who seemed to exist at all hours, always working, always quiet. He was older, with a weathered face and hands that looked surprisingly strong. He always wore a gray hat that matched his gray uniform.

On a whim, Mark stopped. "Jack, did you see anyone come by my office in the last few hours?"

Jack paused the buffer, the hum dying down. He looked at Mark with calm, steady eyes that seemed to see more than they let on. "Can't say I have, Mr. Trenton. People come and go."

Mark hesitated, then pulled the pawn and the note from his pocket. "Someone left me these. It's… strange."

Chapter 2

Jack glanced at the items in Mark's hand, his expression unreadable. He didn't seem surprised or even particularly curious. He just nodded slowly. "A man finds something unexpected on his desk, gets a strange invitation… If it were me, I'd want to know what it meant." He said nothing more, just restarted the buffer, its hum filling the empty hallway once more.

Mark stood there for a moment, the janitor's simple, non-committal words echoing in his mind. He walked into the cool indifference of the night. He got into his car, glancing at the clock. 7:45 PM. He could be home in fifteen minutes, facing the quiet disappointment he knew was waiting. Or he could follow this bizarre, anonymous summons. Against all logic, the spark of curiosity, now fanned by Jack's cryptic encouragement, won out over the dread. Instead of turning toward home, he turned the other way, his mind racing with questions. Who would leave him a chess piece? Who would summon him to a park so late in the evening? It felt absurd, like a scene from a spy movie, but it was also the only thing in his collapsing world that felt like it might lead somewhere new. He drove with a strange sense of purpose, following the familiar route to the old, forgotten patch of green he hadn't visited in years. He killed the engine, and the sudden silence was deafening.

A couple of benches sat under a sprawling oak tree, overlooking a still pond shrouded in a light mist. He walked over and sat down, the quiet, a stark contrast to the alarms in his head. He just breathed, watching the ripples on the water as a duck drifted lazily by. For a moment, the crushing weight on his chest seemed to lift, diffused into the misty air.

A soft, rhythmic scraping sound broke the stillness.

On the adjacent bench sat an older man, perhaps in his late seventies. "Where did he come from?" Mark thought. He was whittling a small piece of wood with a well-worn pocketknife, his movements patient and precise. He had a kind face, etched with lines that spoke of both joy and sorrow. A pair of thick, black plastic-frame glasses sat on his nose. His eyes, focused on his work, seemed to hold a peculiar, knowing twinkle even in the dim light. Mark watched him, mesmerized by the steady, purposeful motion of his hands. The man seemed utterly at peace, a small island of calm in Mark's turbulent sea.

They sat in a comfortable silence for several minutes, the only sounds being the scraping of the knife and the distant murmur of the city. Then, the old man spoke, his voice gentle but clear, without looking up from his carving.

"Being concerned about something is okay," he said, as if continuing a conversation they'd been having for hours. "Being worried about it is not."

Mark froze. The words, so simple and unexpected, landed like a ton of bricks. They were the perfect articulation of the corrosive feeling that had been eating him alive. He looked at the stranger, startled. How could he have known?

The old man finally paused his work, brushing a few stray wood shavings from his trousers. He looked up, and his eyes, clear and direct, met Mark's. There was no pity in them, only a calm, steady understanding.

"Worry is a rocking chair," the man continued, his voice raspy with age but firm with conviction. "Gives you something to do, but it doesn't get you anywhere. Concern, now… concern is different. Concern implies you're getting ready to do something about it. It's the first step toward a solution."

He picked up a fresh piece of wood, turning it over in his calloused hands. "And before you can even begin to find a solution, you have to listen. Really listen. The person doing the job knows more about it than anyone. They know where the real problems are, and often, they know the solution, too. You just have to give them the chance to tell you."

Mark stared, speechless. It was as if this stranger had reached into his chest, pulled out the tangled knot of his anxiety, and laid it bare for him to see. Was this man spying on him? Who is this guy? But the words caught in his throat.

The old man offered a small, knowing smile. "Name's Silas," he said, extending a hand. "Silas Sinclair."

Mark hesitated for a second before taking it. The man's grip was surprisingly firm. "Mark. Mark Trenton."

"Well, Mark Trenton," Silas said, his gaze returning to the pond. "Looks like you've got a choice to make. Are you going to keep rocking in that chair? Or are you going to stand up and walk?"

The question hung in the cool night air, simple, direct, and utterly profound. It was a challenge, but it felt like an invitation. An invitation to a path Mark hadn't realized existed until this very moment.

CHAPTER 3
The Untuned Machine

The words followed Mark into the office the next morning. "Stand up and walk."

He'd slept poorly, but for the first time in months, it wasn't the sleep of a man drowning in a sea of worry. It was the restless sleep of a man contemplating a difficult journey. Silas's distinction between worry and concern had replayed in his mind. Worry was passive, a victim's emotion. Concern was active, the posture of a leader.

On his calendar for 10:00 AM was a meeting with Sarah Jenkins, the lead engineer on Chimera's primary processing unit. The meeting's purpose, as far as his boss Richard was concerned, was for Mark to 'light a fire under her.' The data showed her team's output was slow and riddled with errors. Mark had been ready to march into that meeting armed with charts and a stern lecture.

But today, he was concerned and a little more open to listening.

On his way in, Mark had stopped at "The Daily Grind," a local coffee shop with a warm, inviting atmosphere. He'd bought two coffees in a cardboard carrier and walked into the office, the rich aroma cutting through the stale, recycled air. He balanced them carefully as he walked to Sarah's cubicle. She looked up as he approached, her expression already defensive, as if bracing for impact.

"Morning, Sarah," he said, offering the carrier. "Got a minute? I was hoping we could talk. That little huddle room is free."

The surprise on her face was evident. She took one of the cups, her fingers brushing the warm cardboard. "Uh, sure. Thanks."

Mark liked to meet places other than his office, because if he needed to leave or end a meeting, it gave him a place to retreat. The huddle room was a small glass box, offering privacy but not secrecy. Anyone walking by could see them talking. They sat down, the coffee cups forming a small barrier between them. He didn't start with the metrics. He didn't start with the delays. He decided, for once, to just listen.

"Tell me how it's really going, Sarah," he said simply.

She gave him a wary look, as if expecting a trap. "It's… challenging. We're working through the issues."

"I'm not here to blame anyone," Mark said, leaning forward. "I'm here to understand. Help me see what you're seeing."

As he looked at her—at the dark circles under her eyes, the tension in her jaw, the way her fingers nervously tapped her coffee cup—he could see the evidence that something was wrong. He had only seen charts and data points. She was living the problem. He was in meetings, shuffling papers and promises. She was on the front lines, fighting a battle he couldn't even perceive. At that moment, Silas's words hung in his mind: "No one knows the job better than the person doing it."

It was a simple idea, but it changed everything. It shifted him from judge to student.

The shift in his own perspective, the silent acknowledgment of her expertise, must have shown on his face. Her shoulders slumped, not in defeat, but in a weary release of tension. She took a deep breath.

"Mark, we have multiple problems, but it's not the designs. It's not my team," she said, her voice low and urgent. "The tools we have in the shop aren't accurate enough and they keep breaking down. We tried to save money by getting cheaper brands, but now it's costing us time."

Mark looked at her with some compassion and said, "Yes, let's not try to save money on tools. We need them to get the job done. However, things like nuts and bolts or parts based on a spec, we should be able to save money on these."

Sarah slumped in her chair, "Well, that's the other problem, our parts are not up to spec. They're garbage."

She pulled her phone from her pocket and slid it across the table. It showed a series of emails and photos. "This is from VexTech, our supplier. We're supposed to be getting micro-controllers rated for 1.2 gigahertz. The last three shipments? Most of them can't even sustain 1.0 without overheating. They're either factory seconds or outright counterfeits. We spend half our time just testing and rejecting parts. We're not building; we're just doing quality control for a supplier that doesn't care."

She scrolled to another email. "I've flagged this to VexTech three times. This was their last response."

Mark read the curt, dismissive reply, which essentially told Sarah to re-read the technical specifications and stop wasting their time.

"Why didn't you bring this to me?" Mark asked, a cold dread creeping up his spine.

Sarah looked away, staring into her coffee. "Honestly? Because everyone is looking for a scapegoat. I figured if I pointed the finger at a supplier, it would just look like I was making excuses for my team's performance. I thought I could… I don't know… work around it."

Mark felt a flush of shame. She was right. He had been so focused on the internal metrics, on Richard's pressure, on David's snide remarks, that he'd forgotten to look at the whole picture. He'd been trying to tune an engine without checking if it had any fuel.

He now understood the real problem. The source of the rot. But this knowledge wasn't a relief; it was a new, more terrifying weight. VexTech wasn't just any supplier. They were Richard's pet vendor, a company he'd brought in himself, constantly praising their "aggressive pricing" and "can-do attitude."

To challenge VexTech was to challenge Richard's judgment. It was to walk directly into a political minefield.

He had stood up from the rocking chair, just as Silas had challenged him to do. But as he looked at Sarah's exhausted but hopeful face, he realized his first step forward had landed him on the edge of a cliff.

CHAPTER 4

The Power of a Question

The VexTech problem burned in Mark's mind like a hot coal. It was the kind of problem that could end a career, a political grenade with the pin already pulled. But before he could even begin to think about how to defuse it, he was summoned to another fire.

"Conference room, ten minutes," Richard's email barked. "Urgent: Competitive Strategy Session."

Mark walked into the room to a scene of barely controlled panic. The new competitor, a nimble startup named Apex Solutions, had just announced a new feature that directly targeted Innovate Dynamics's core client base. The news had sent shockwaves through the leadership team.

"They're eating our lunch!" Richard said, pacing in front of the whiteboard. "They're faster, they're cheaper, and now they're out-innovating us. What are we going to do?"

David, the head of marketing, stepped forward, practically vibrating with self-importance. He tapped a marker on the board. "It's a perception war, Richard. We need to hit back, and hit back hard. I'm proposing a multi-platform campaign. We'll saturate the market. We'll offer a 20% discount to any Apex client who switches to us. We'll fight fire with fire."

The room murmured in agreement. It was a plan—an aggressive, tangible plan. It felt like action. But to Mark, it felt like desperation. He thought of Sarah, of the faulty components, of the product they couldn't even build properly. Discounting a broken product was like putting a sale sign on a sinking ship.

A few days ago, Mark would have stayed silent, overwhelmed by the consensus. But the conversation with Silas echoed in his mind, followed by the raw truth from Sarah. He was seeing a roomful of executives about to spend millions of dollars based on fear and guesswork.

"Hold on," Mark said. The room fell silent, surprised by his interruption.

He walked to the whiteboard. "David, you say they're cheaper. How much cheaper?"

David blinked. "Well, significantly. They're undercutting us across the board."

A thought crystallized in Mark's mind: The trouble with people who don't know what they're talking about is that they don't know when to stop. Mark pressed his advantage. "How much is 'significantly'? By 5%? 10%? 25%? What's the actual number?"

David stammered, "I'd have to get the exact figures from my team…"

"And you say they're faster," Mark continued, turning to the head of sales. "What's their average deployment time compared to ours? Do we have data on that? And what about their customer support? What's their average ticket resolution time?"

The room was filled with blank stares. They had feelings. They had fears. They had no numbers.

A new clarity washed over Mark. It was another epiphany, a piece of wisdom clicking into place with the satisfying certainty of a well-machined part. If you can't describe something using numbers, you don't know what you are talking about. They were all just talking.

"We're trying to solve a problem we haven't even defined," Mark said, his voice gaining confidence. He looked at Richard. "Before we spend a dime on a marketing war, we need to ask the right questions. The problem isn't 'Apex is beating us.' That's a conclusion. The problem is a set of facts we don't have yet."

He uncapped a blue marker. "The first question is: Where, specifically, are we losing, and by how much? The second is: Where are they genuinely better, and where are they just perceived as better? And the third, and most important question is: Where are they weak?"

He felt a profound shift in his own thinking. He wasn't just repeating something he'd been told; he was understanding it from the inside out. The answer to every problem lies in a properly crafted question.

Richard had stopped pacing. He stared at the whiteboard, at the simple, direct questions Mark had written. It was as if Mark had cut through a fog of panic with a sharp knife.

"Get the numbers," Richard said, his voice low but firm. He wasn't looking at David anymore. He was looking at Mark. "I want a full analysis. Dig into their customer reviews, their support forums, everything. Find their weakness." He paused. "David, hold off on the campaign blitz. Mark, I want this on my desk in forty-eight hours."

Mark nodded, a feeling of quiet triumph mixing with a new wave of pressure. He had won the battle, but in doing so, he had publicly sidelined David and taken on a massive new responsibility. And all the while, the unexploded bomb of the VexTech situation was still ticking in his pocket. He had just volunteered to fight a war on two fronts.

CHAPTER 5

The Hasty Rush

The glow from the victory in the strategy session was short-lived, a brief ceasefire in a war now being fought on two fronts. The 48-hour deadline for the Apex analysis was a ticking clock in one ear, while the VexTech problem was the low-grade fever of an untreated wound. He slumped into his chair, the weight of it all pressing down, and his eyes fell upon his desk. He had placed the two pawns there earlier. One was the original, pale-colored piece that he had found the other night. Next to it was the new dark one Silas had carved for him during their first talk. He had set them facing each other, two lone soldiers on a battlefield, poised and waiting for the command to engage.

He stared at the two small figures, grappling with the symbolism. Why pawns? Why not a more powerful piece? He couldn't shake the feeling that Silas was implying something profound about his situation. Was he just a pawn in a much larger game? Perhaps he was reminding him that even the smallest pieces have a critical role to play. The thought didn't just stir anxiety; it coiled in his stomach like a cold snake, a feeling that he was missing a crucial part of the puzzle.

The Hasty Rush

An email notification flashed on his screen, breaking the spell. The subject line was from Richard: "FWD: URGENT: Vex-Tech Limited Time Offer."

Mark's heart sank as he read it. It was a formal proposal from VexTech, offering a massive 20% discount on a bulk order of their micro-controllers—the very components Sarah had proven were faulty. Richard's message was blunt:

Mark, this is a huge opportunity. The cost savings on this bulk order would put the Chimera project significantly under budget. VexTech says the offer is only good until the end of the day. Let's not be penny-wise here. I need your sign-off by 4 PM so we can lock this in. This is a big win for us.

It was a trap. A beautiful, gold-plated, budget-saving trap. Richard, blinded by the dollar signs, was pressuring him to make a hasty choice, to commit to a year's worth of components that could be utterly worthless. The weight of it all—the dueling deadlines, the mysterious pawns, the pressure from his boss—felt crushing. He needed advice. He needed clarity. He needed the calm, steady wisdom of the old man in the park.

Driven by a desperation that overrode all logic, Mark grabbed his keys and left the office.

The park was quiet, the afternoon sun filtering through the leaves. He saw him immediately. He was just now sitting down on the bench where he was before, opening his bag to whittle a small piece of wood. A wave of relief washed over Mark.

"Silas," Mark began, sinking onto the adjacent bench without introduction. He barely knew the man, but he laid out the whole impossible situation—the pressure from Richard, the bad components, the end-of-day deadline. "He wants an answer now. If I say yes, I could be poisoning the entire project. If I say no, I'm turning down a massive cost-saving, and Richard will see it as me being difficult and indecisive."

Silas didn't look up from his carving. "Sounds like they're trying to rush you."

"They are," Mark said. "I feel like I'm trapped."

"Then the answer is simple," Silas said, his knife making a soft, scraping sound. "When you're being pressured to make a quick choice, the answer is always 'no.'"

Mark stared at him. "Just… no? That's it?"

"That's it," Silas confirmed. He finally paused his work and looked at Mark, his eyes clear and direct. "Saying 'no' isn't a rejection of the deal, Mark. It's a rejection of their timeline. It's a tool that reclaims your control. The person rushing you is doing it for their benefit, not yours. They're creating a false sense of urgency, hoping you'll make a mistake. When you say 'no,' you stop their game. You force them to play on your timeline, which gives you the one thing you need most: time to solve your problems."

The wisdom of it was so simple, so profound, that Mark felt a knot of tension in his chest loosen. It wasn't about fighting Richard; it was about solving their problems without creating more.

Mark turned toward Silas with a pleading look in his eyes, "Silas, are you here often? I feel like I could use your advice more than I'd like to admit."

Silas put his hand on a wadded-up gray hat next to him and gave a mysterious smile. "I'm here as much as I need to be."

"But what if I need you and you're not here?" Mark pressed, a new anxiety surfacing. "Could we… I don't know… set up regular time to meet? Maybe we could meet weekly?"

Silas chuckled, a warm, dry sound. "Just meet me here, Mark."

"But I don't want to drive all this way just to sit and stare at the ducks by myself," Mark protested politely.

"Perhaps," Silas said, his eyes twinkling, "staring at the ducks by yourself is exactly what you'll need on that day." He saw the look on Mark's face and his expression softened. "Don't you worry. If you really need me, I'll be here."

Mark felt a sense of doubt. How could he know when he would be needed? Mark stood up, a little frustrated by Silas's odd commitment. Was Silas homeless? He needed to get back to work. As he turned to leave, Silas held out his hand. In his palm was another freshly carved pawn.

Mark hesitated. "Why do you keep giving me these pawns?" he asked, his voice full of confusion.

Silas just smiled, a knowing look in his eyes. "All the pieces will come together in the end, Mark. You'll see."

Mark took the small wooden pawn, its familiar weight a comfort in his hand. The words were cryptic, but strangely reassuring. He now had a reason to push back on the Vex-Tech deal and focus on the real threat: Apex. The first step was to say no. The second step was to build a team and figure out what made their competitor tick. He headed back to the office, not with a solution, but with a strategy, ready to face this storm.

CHAPTER 6

The Leaves or The Tree

Mark hit the send button and watched as his "no" response to VexTech's offer went on its way. He hoped Silas was right. Pushing back on this could cost him his job. Then he went about the office recruiting members of various departments to be on his research team.

Before long, Mark quickly gathered his team of sharp, young analysts in a conference room. The space soon became a chaotic mess of whiteboards, spreadsheets, and half-empty coffee cups.

The problem wasn't a lack of information; it was a flood. And his team, determined to be thorough, was focused on making the flood bigger.

"Mark, I've found a new angle," Jeff, a new junior analyst, said, his eyes wide with the thrill of the data hunt. "There are third-party logistics firms that publish quarterly shipping reports. If we purchase the raw data, we can cross-reference it with Apex's supplier locations and maybe build a model of their potential supply chain vulnerabilities. The data set costs a few thousand dollars, but it would give us a whole new stream of information."

Mark felt a spike of anxiety. They were spending all their time and energy finding new ways to collect data, but they weren't making any progress processing what they already had. They were sharpening a dozen pencils, but hadn't written a single word. He tried to steer them back. "That's a creative idea, Jeff, but we have terabytes of data already. We don't need more streams; we need to find the river. The answer is in what we have."

Mark looked at their blank faces and realized they weren't just collecting data; they were hiding in it. They were so focused on the process that they'd lost the purpose. They could see the leaves, but they couldn't envision the tree. All they could see were the raw numbers.

After a long day, Mark left the office in a huff. He walked through the sprawling parking lot to his car, parked in his usual spot—backed into the space. He always parked right next to a concrete light pole base. It was a habit he'd picked up years ago. He always felt more alert when he arrived than when he left work. When he entered the office he was fresh. When he left, especially on days like this, his thoughts were on everything other than the act of backing out of a parking space. It was safer. And parking next to the barricade meant one less side of his car for people to bump into. It was a small thing, but he had enough other stressful things to deal with in life.

He got into the car, his mind still churning. He felt like they were getting nowhere. Maybe he should have never challenged David and ended up with this 48-hour responsibility. Why did he feel the need to stick his neck out? Then he thought of Silas again. He said he would be there when he needed him, but would he be there now? Surely, he wouldn't be there all day.

Mark's car pulled into the parking lot. He looked out by the tree and he saw a figure on the bench. Was it Silas? Mark stepped out and a gust of wind whipped his hair. Mark stared at the leaves of the tree dancing as he approached the bench.

"You look like a man trying to count all the leaves on that oak tree," Silas said without looking up.

"Worse," Mark sighed, sinking onto the adjacent bench. "I have a team trying to invent new kinds of leaves to count, and we have to present the whole tree tomorrow. They're so focused on the planning and collecting that the actual analysis—the part that matters—is going to be a last-minute, panicked mess."

Silas chuckled. "Ah, yes. The old corporate two-step. It reminds me of the saying we had on the factory floor, born from watching overly complex government specs get built. They measure with a micrometer, mark with chalk, and cut with an axe. People pour all their energy and passion into the planning phase, gathering information. But the planning takes so long that by the time it comes to actually make the decision, they've lost steam. All that careful, upfront work gets wasted because the final cut is sloppy. It's a tremendous amount of effort just to get a bad result."

The words hit Mark like a slap to the face. That was exactly what was happening. His team was measuring with a micrometer, and he was heading for a rushed, sloppy cut with an axe.

"It's such a waste of resources," Mark muttered. "Time, money, people's energy…"

"Speaking of resources," Silas said, pausing his whittling. "I had a manager once who would spend every last dime in his budget by the end of the year, buying things we didn't even need. He was terrified by the 'use it or lose it' mindset. I finally had to explain to him that when working with a budget, you don't adopt the 'use it or lose it' concept. Returning the unspent funds shows the front office you're responsible. The next year, when he needed a big increase for a new machine, they gave it to him without blinking. If your team doesn't waste money, it will pay off. The Bible says that if you are faithful with a little, you will be entrusted with much."

Silas then held up a rough, uncut block of wood in one hand and the nearly finished knight in the other. "But the real issue is this. You have to remember that many people cannot envision from a prototype or drawings. They can't see the finished product. All they can see is this," he said, gesturing with the block of wood. "They see the raw data, they can't see the knight—the simple, powerful insight that will win the battle. They get scared because they can't grasp what the final answer is supposed to look like. People in this situation will try to focus on the smaller of the two problems. So they try to get more data instead of analyzing it."

Mark stared at the two pieces of wood. The problem wasn't his team's incompetence; it was his failure to communicate the vision. He hadn't shown them what the knight they were carving would look like.

"What do I do?" Mark asked. "I don't even know what the knight is yet."

"You're the leader," Silas said simply. "Your job isn't to know the answer. Your job is to define what you are looking for. You are looking for a simple, clear weakness or a single, powerful strength. Stop them from focusing on measuring and have them prepare to make their cut. Tell them the goal is to cut off the irrelevant data to identify the knight. Together, you need to find what is hiding in the block of wood."

Mark left the park not with a solution, but with a new strategy for his team. He knew he had to walk back into that war room, call a halt to the endless data collection, and find a new way to describe the shape of the victory they were all searching for.

CHAPTER 7

The Story of the Cup Dispenser

The next morning, Mark was walking down the hall when he saw David holding court in a glass-walled conference room. He had called an "urgent" all-hands meeting for the marketing department to discuss a new policy for reserving conference rooms. It was a trivial issue, but David treated it with the gravity of a national security crisis. Mark paused, watching the spectacle. It was a masterful, if pathetic, performance. The real, systemic issue was the company's flawed marketing strategy, a problem David wanted everyone to forget.

At that moment, Mark remembered what Silas had said last night, "People tend to concentrate on the smaller of two problems." David was creating a tiny, manageable fire to distract everyone from the inferno he had started. It was creative and tactful, but David wasn't trying to help the company. He was just trying to take the heat off himself. Mark filed the tactic away. A tool for diversion, he thought, could be powerful if aimed at the right target.

The Story of the Cup Dispenser

As Mark came to the research team's conference room, he slowed. His team was pouring in, and letting them go first was the least he could do to show them respect for all their hard work. When he came into the room, he had a new ambition from his talk with Silas.

Mark launched off their time together, saying, "It's a new day, and we need to find a way to cut through this data to reveal what we need from it."

Nevertheless, hours later, the sun was lower in the sky, and the atmosphere in the conference room was thick with frustration. Whiteboards were covered in dead-end diagrams, and his research team was staring blankly at a sea of spreadsheets. They were drowning in data.

"We're just going in circles," Jeff said, rubbing his eyes. "We have all this data, but it's not telling us anything new. Apex is cheaper and faster. That's it."

James had been quietly listening to people for the last couple of hours. He was bald on top and wore a plaid button-up shirt. When he spoke up, the room went silent. "I had a friend who was running a small factory that made cup dispensers. The standard sizes were four, six, and eight ounces. That's all anyone made. One day, my friend got a phone call from a man whom he had never heard of before. That man asked him if he could make a ten-ounce dispenser. Now, every other manufacturer he'd called had turned him down flat, some of them rudely. They gave him a speech about industry standards and tooling costs. They talked, but they didn't listen." James looked at everyone who had been talking constantly for the last couple of hours, "The Lord gave you two ears and one mouth. We ought to use them in that proportion."

The group was shocked by James's being so blunt, but before they could retaliate, he continued. "My friend listened to that man. He told him he'd check the tooling and call him back. So he walked out to the shop, and it turned out they only needed a few simple modifications. Next, he called him back and got an order for samples. Soon, he had a massive order when that man liked them. That man became one of his best customers. And a few years later, when ten-ounce cups became the new standard, my friend was the only one ready for it. All because he took five minutes to listen instead of giving a speech."

Chloe, who was from David's department, looked shocked. Everyone thought she was going to explode at James's rebuke as she shook her artistically highlighted red-streaked hair. Then she burst out, "Wow, wow, maybe that is it! Apex tells a good story that sticks in your head. It's not just a bunch of bullet points from a marketing speech—the kind you hear today and are gone tomorrow. It's got us all captivated! But maybe we shouldn't be listening to 'their story'. Maybe we should be listening to their customers?"

Mark raised a brow, "Chloe, you were reading their social media posts, right? Is something standing out to you?"

Chloe continued, "We're so focused on their official marketing, but their social media comments are a disaster. It's not about features; it's about follow-through. People are furious that they can't get a real person on the phone. Apex is making a speech about their product, but they're not listening to their own customers."

The room was silent for a moment as everyone digested this. How had they overlooked this?

The Story of the Cup Dispenser

"So," Mark said, walking to the whiteboard and taking some notes. "They're making a promise about their product, but they're breaking a more fundamental promise about service. They are captivating everyone with one story, but we can captivate people with another."

He looked around at the team, seeing the idea begin to spark in their eyes. Chloe said, "So, we don't play their game. We don't fight on price. We find our opportunity in their failure. What if our greatest strength isn't in our product, but in our people?"

Jeff caught on, his excitement shifting from the raw data to the strategy. "Where their product fails, ours proves its strength."

"Exactly!" Mark said, "But we can do even more. We could make every business surprise a good one. People expect their delivery on time. They expect the product to work. That's the baseline. But what if we promise delivery in five days and it shows up in three? What if they call customer service expecting a fight and get a real, helpful person who solves their problem on the first try? We don't just meet expectations; we shatter them. We underpromise and we overperform."

A new energy filled the room. The team wasn't just looking at numbers anymore; they were seeing the story. They saw the path forward—not one of being cheaper, but of being trustworthy, reliable, and surprisingly human.

Mark stared at the whiteboard, the path now forming. He had less than twenty-four hours left, but for the first time, he knew what he was looking for. He wasn't just looking for a weakness to exploit in Apex; he was looking for a story for themselves that could captivate the market. Yet he still felt uneasy. The faulty parts from VexTech could spoil their story.

CHAPTER 8

The Shaken Sack

Mark's report on Apex Solutions landed on Richard's desk with a soft thud forty-seven hours later. It was a masterclass in data-driven analysis, revealing that while Apex was indeed cheaper, their customer support was a dumpster fire. Their online reviews were a litany of unanswered emails, unresolved tickets, and frustrated clients. Their weakness was clear. The path forward, focusing on superior service and reliability, was a strategy Richard embraced immediately.

The success elevated Mark's status overnight. He went from being the manager of a failing project to the company's new strategic guru. The shift was obvious. Colleagues who used to nod curtly in the hallway now stopped to chat. And Richard, his boss, saw him as the go-to guy for putting out fires.

Which is why Bill, the head of the logistics department, was now standing in Mark's doorway, wringing his hands.

"Mark, got a second?" Bill asked, his face a mask of desperation. "I've got a real mess on my hands."

Chapter 8

"Come on in, Bill," Mark said, gesturing to the chair in front of his desk.

Bill collapsed into the chair and launched into his story. "It's Tom and Jerry. No, not the cartoon, I wish. It's Tom Peterson and Jerry Fikes. They're my two best forklift operators, but they hate each other's guts. It's been simmering for months, but yesterday it boiled over. They had a shouting match in the middle of the warehouse floor in front of everyone. Now the whole department is choosing sides. Productivity is in the tank. I don't know what to do. I need you to talk to them. Lay down the law."

As Bill spoke, Mark felt a strange sense of detachment. He tried to think, What would Silas say? But it wasn't Silas's voice that came to mind. Instead, it was the gruff voice of his first boss, a grizzled old factory foreman named Gus. Years ago, a panicked supervisor had tried to get Gus to discipline two feuding machinists. Gus had just laughed and said, "Son, that there is a shaken sack. He can't solve his own problem, so he shook up the skunks inside and is trying to hand you the bag. Don't you ever take the bag."

The memory, long dormant, surfaced with startling clarity. That's exactly what was happening. Bill was avoiding his responsibility, handing Mark a sack full of angry skunks, hoping he would be the one to open it and get sprayed. The wisdom was the same kind Silas would offer—practical, grounded, and painted with a vivid picture.

With everyone looking up to him, Mark wanted to play the hero. He wanted to wade into the conflict and impress everyone with his skills, but he knew better. This wasn't his problem to solve; it was his problem to guide.

The Shaken Sack

"That sounds tough, Bill," Mark said calmly. "What have you tried so far?"

Bill deflated slightly. "Well, I told them both to knock it off. To act like professionals."

"And how did that work out?"

"It didn't. They just glared at each other and went back to work. The tension is even worse now."

"Okay," Mark said, leaning forward. "Let's forget about Tom and Jerry for a second. What's the outcome you want?"

"I want them to stop fighting so we can get back to work!"

"That's the short-term fix," Mark countered. "What's the real goal? A productive team? A respectful workplace? What does the department look like when this is solved permanently?"

Bill was silent for a moment, forced to think beyond the immediate crisis. "I guess… I want a team that can handle disagreements without shutting down the whole warehouse."

"Good," Mark said. "That's a goal. Now, you're the one who has to lead them there." He saw the panic return to Bill's eyes and held up a hand. "But I'll give you the tools. You said the shouting match was public, right?"

Bill nodded.

"Then the solution has to start publicly. But the discipline? That's private. It's a simple rule, Bill, but it's powerful: When you congratulate someone, do it publicly. If you're chewing them out, do it in private. You need to get Tom and Jerry in a room, just the three of you. No audience. And you let them have their say, one at a time."

Mark continued, "But before that, you address the whole department. Not to point fingers, but to reaffirm the standard. You tell them that you, as their leader, failed to maintain a respectful workplace, and that it stops now. You make the public correction for the public mistake. You shoulder the blame, Bill. That's how you get their respect back."

Bill stared at Mark, a mixture of fear and dawning understanding on his face. He hadn't been given a solution; he'd been given a compass and a map. He was still the one who had to walk the path.

"Okay," Bill said, standing up slowly. "Okay. I can do that."

As Bill walked out, looking more like a leader and less like a victim, Mark felt a sense of satisfaction. But it was fleeting. He glanced across the office and saw David, his marketing rival, watching him from his glass-walled office. There was no warmth in David's gaze, only the cold, calculating look of a predator that had been momentarily outmaneuvered.

Mark had just taught another manager how to handle a sack of skunks, but he knew the biggest, most venomous snake in the building was still coiled, waiting for him to make a single misstep on the VexTech problem. And that was a fight he knew he couldn't delegate.

That night, as Mark was packing his briefcase, he saw Jack emptying the trash cans nearby. The janitor moved with a quiet efficiency that Mark was beginning to admire. Jack paused, leaning on his cart, and nodded toward David's empty office.

The Shaken Sack

"Amazing what you can see when you stop looking at the mess and start looking at the people," Jack said, his voice low. He wiped his hands on a gray rag, and Mark noticed for a brief second that they were thick with calluses, like the hands of a man who worked with more than just a mop and broom. Then, as quietly as he had appeared, Jack pushed his cart down the hall and disappeared around the corner.

CHAPTER 9

The Threads of Trust

A few days after Mark had coached Bill through his department's crisis, he saw David showing a picture on his phone to Bill from logistics by the coffee machine.

"Pulled this monster out of the lake this weekend," David was boasting, his voice loud enough for anyone nearby to hear. "A real fighter."

"Wow, David! That's a huge bass," Bill said, genuinely impressed. "Where'd you snag him?"

David gave a slight, almost imperceptible shrug and glanced away for a fraction of a second before looking back at Bill. "Oh, you know. Just over at Lake Killarney. They're practically jumping into the boat over there." He then saw Mark and his expression shifted, the boastful smile replaced by brows pulled down slightly.

"Mark, hey," he said, his voice oozing false friendliness. "Things just got a bit heated the other day. Sorry about that." He clapped Mark on the shoulder.

Mark looked at him, at the smile that didn't reach his eyes, and the casual, dismissive phrase. "The other day?" Mark thought, "Was he talking about last week or a couple of days ago?" An image of Silas flashed in his mind, the old man's voice calm and clear. When someone is smiling as they say "I'm sorry," or if they use a catchphrase like "sorry about that," they are not sorry. It wasn't a cynical thought; it was just a clear observation. David wasn't apologizing for his actions; he was annoyed they hadn't worked.

"Thanks, David," Mark said, his voice neutral, and walked away. The encounter solidified a new resolve. He was learning that building trust wasn't just about being trustworthy himself; it was about discerning who was worthy of his trust in return.

This new lens changed how he saw everything. He couldn't afford to be blindsided again. He started actively seeking out the people who weren't afraid to tell him the truth, creating an informal "council of truth" with Sarah and Chloe. "I don't need yes-men," he told them during one of their coffee huddles. "I need people who will tell me when I'm about to step on a landmine. You need people around you who will voice their true opinion."

He also started to change his own methods after his regular times with Silas. The data his team had uncovered about Apex was powerful, but it was still raw and could be organized better. Mark wanted to lock himself in his office and wrestle it into a presentation by himself. However, remembering Silas's advice to delegate, he called over Jeff, the sharp junior analyst. He pulled up the tangled spreadsheets.

"Jeff," he said, "this feels messy to me. I'm too close to it. The story is in here somewhere, but we need to tell it in a way Richard and the board will understand instantly. Take a look at this and tell me if you see a more elegant way to present this information."

A week later, Jeff came back with a brilliant, streamlined dashboard concept. It was better than anything Mark would have designed. At the next team meeting, Mark had Jeff present the idea. "Jeff's had a breakthrough on the weekly reporting," he announced. The team loved it, and Jeff, who had never been singled out for praise before, was beaming. Mark felt a quiet satisfaction. He hadn't just improved a process; he had empowered an employee. He had learned a principle that he should plant the seed of an idea in others and watch it grow because a project has a better chance of success when the person doing it is involved with the idea.

That evening, he went to his familiar spot at the park. He told Silas about his observations and small experiments in trust-building.

"I just don't trust David, Silas," Mark admitted, his frustration evident. "It feels like he cares more about his own reputation than he does about the company. He's willing to mislead people and twist the truth to make himself look good. It's like he's stealing focus and resources for his own benefit."

"That's a sharp observation," Silas said with a nod of approval. "You're right to be wary. It reminds me of a lesson a friend of mine with a retail business learned the hard way. He caught one of his clerks intentionally short-changing a customer. When he confronted him, the clerk protested, saying the extra money was a bonus for the business. My friend fired him on the spot."

The Threads of Trust

"Even though the clerk was trying to help the business?" Mark asked.

"Especially then," Silas said, his gaze firm. "My friend knew that a person who will steal for you, will eventually steal from you. A thief is a thief. Their moral code isn't situational. The same applies to a person who lies. A man who lies for you will just as easily lie to you when it suits him. A man who tells you where he catches fish or finds mushrooms will lie about other things, too. You can't build anything real on a foundation of stealing and lies."

Mark nodded, the principle solidifying his instincts about David. David's self-serving agenda wasn't just a difference in style; it was a threat. He was playing his own game, and Mark knew he had to watch him more closely than ever. He then told Silas about delegating to Jeff and trying to be more patient.

"That's good," Silas said with a nod of approval. "But you have to be patient with it. You have to make haste slowly." He told Mark a story about a time his factory got a huge rush order. In their hurry, they skipped a final curing step on a batch of rubber gaskets. They shipped on time, but a week later, the entire shipment came back—the gaskets had all cracked. "We had to redo the whole order, cost us twice as much, and we almost lost the customer. We were in such a hurry to get there, we forgot to make sure the wheels were on the wagon."

Silas went on, a humorous glint in his eye. "It's a lesson in caution. A friend of mine who sat on the board of a hospital once told me they were going to name a new wing after a big donor. I told him, 'Don't you ever name something in honor of someone that is still alive.' They can still embarrass you. Well, they didn't listen. A year later, that donor was all over the news for tax evasion. They had to pay a fortune to take his name off the building."

The stories, as always, settled into Mark's mind, connecting threads of wisdom. Be patient. Be prudent. Pay attention.

As he was leaving, Mark's phone buzzed. It was a text from David. It read: "I have the perfect solution." It sent a jolt of ice through his veins. "What was David up to now?"

CHAPTER 10

The Unread Sign

The two little wooden rooks sat on the corner of Mark's desk standing guard over the papers and notes spread across it. In the week since his victories with the Apex report and Bill's feuding forklift operators, he had started seeing the world differently. It was as if he'd been living in a black-and-white movie that was slowly bleeding into color. He noticed things he'd been blind to before—the small, subtle currents of culture that shaped the entire company.

He saw it that afternoon as he walked through the main lobby. On the wall, gleaming in expensive, brushed aluminum, was the company's mission statement: "Innovate Dynamics: Engineering Synergistic Paradigms for a New Tomorrow." He'd walked past it a thousand times. Today, for the first time, he actually tried to read it. The font was a wispy, elegant script, so full of loops and flourishes that it was nearly illegible. It was corporate art, designed to be seen but not understood. What did it even mean? It was gibberish. Expensive, unreadable gibberish.

A wave of disgust washed over him. This sign, in its own way, was as much a part of the problem as VexTech's faulty parts. It was a lie, pretending to be a principle.

His irritation grew when he stopped by the mailroom. Pinned to the bulletin board was a memo from accounting about a new, extended warranty program—a genuinely good thing for their customers. But the headline, in bold, aggressive letters, read: "FAILURE TO COMPLY WITH NEW WARRANTY SUBMISSION PROTOCOLS WILL RESULT IN CLAIM DENIAL."

It was an announcement about a benefit, phrased as a threat. It was an invitation to a party that started with a warning not to scuff the floors.

These were small things, but they were everything. They were the symptoms of a lazy, negative, inward-facing culture. He felt a familiar pull, the desire to drive to the park and lay this new frustration at Silas's feet.

He found the old man in his usual spot, the late afternoon sun filtering through the leaves of the oak tree.

"You look like a man who's just discovered a new species of insect he doesn't like," Silas commented as Mark sat down.

Mark explained what he'd seen—the unreadable mission statement and the hostile warranty memo. "It's just... lazy," Mark finished, frustrated. "It's careless. It feels like we're actively working against our own customers."

Silas chuckled, a dry, rustling sound. "What you're seeing, Mark, is that the little things aren't little. You're seeing the soul of the company. And right now, it's got a real scowl on its face."

The Unread Sign

He pointed his whittling knife at Mark. "Let me ask you something. You go to a store, you buy your things, and the clerk says, 'Is that all?' How does that make you feel?"

"I don't know," Mark said. "Like they want me to be done so they can get to the next person."

"Exactly," Silas said. "It's a negative question. It closes the door. Now, what if that same clerk smiled and asked, 'Would there be anything else for you today?' See the difference? One is a dismissal, the other is an invitation. One is negative, the other is positive. It's a tiny change in words, but a huge change in feeling."

Silas leaned back, his point made. "It's simple, Mark. Make your signs and logos readable. And make your statements positive. You want people to feel good about dealing with you, not like they're solving a puzzle or about to get in trouble. You have to think about the person who doesn't already know what your sign says. You have to write for the customer, not for the accounting department."

The wisdom resonated so deeply with Mark. It seemed so obvious that Mark felt like the company should have seen it long ago. They had been so focused on the big, complex machinery of the business that they had ignored the user manual.

"I'm going to change it," Mark said, a new resolve hardening in his voice. "I'm going to propose a company-wide 'Clarity and Positivity' initiative. Rewrite everything, from the mission statement to our customer service scripts."

"Good," Silas said with a nod. "You're starting to lead."

Mark left the park feeling energized, his mind buzzing with ideas. He would draft a proposal for Richard first thing in the morning. This wasn't just about fixing a sign; this was about reframing their entire strategy. It was about turning outward to the customer instead of inward at their own processes.

He walked into the office the next day, proposal in hand, ready to make his case. As he approached Richard's office, the door opened. David stepped out, a smug smile playing on his lips. He held a copy of the aggressive warranty memo in his hand, tapping it thoughtfully against his chin.

"Morning, Mark," David said, his eyes glinting with malice. "Headed in to see Richard? I was just telling him how much I admire the accounting department's firm hand. In these tough times, we need to make sure our customers know we mean business."

CHAPTER 11

The Golden Silence

David's words hung in the air like poison gas. Mark felt a surge of anger, hot and sharp, but he forced it down. Arguing with David was like wrestling a pig in mud; you both get dirty, and the pig likes it. He gave a tight, noncommittal nod and stepped past him into Richard's office.

"Close the door," Richard said without looking up from his computer.

Mark's proposal for the 'Clarity and Positivity' initiative felt flimsy in his hand. David had already poisoned the well.

"Richard, I've been thinking about our company messaging…" Mark began.

"Later," Richard cut him off, finally swiveling in his chair. His expression was grim. "David's right about one thing. We need to project strength. Optics. Which brings me to the real fire. VexTech."

The name landed like a stone in Mark's gut.

"How could you turn down that offer? And why is Sarah Jenkins from your team sending those emails?" Richard continued, his voice dangerously calm. "She's claiming their components are out of spec. VexTech is our premier partner, Mark. I brought them in myself. This makes us look bad. It makes me look bad."

"The components are out of spec and buying lots of bad parts won't save us anything," Mark said, his own voice steady. "Sarah has documented proof."

"Then handle it," Richard snapped. "I don't want to hear about it again. I've arranged a call for you and Sarah with their lead account manager this afternoon. Make this problem go away. And Mark," he added, his eyes narrowing, "this is a partnership, not a lawsuit. Be diplomatic and get me that deal back."

The message was clear: fix the unfixable problem, but don't upset the person causing it.

The hours leading up to the call were agonizing. This was the VexTech fight he'd been dreading, and now he was walking into it with his hands tied. He needed a different kind of tool. He found himself once again in his car, driving to the park.

Silas was wearing gray pants and pulling his wood from a bag to start carving. Mark didn't even sit down. He paced in front of the bench, recounting the impossible situation Richard had put him in.

"So I'm supposed to negotiate with a supplier who is actively lying to us, but I can't accuse them of lying or make them angry," Mark finished, throwing his hands up in exasperation.

Silas finished a delicate cut on the piece he was carving then looked up. "I had a friend in Human Resources once. A sharp woman. When she'd interview a promising candidate, she'd get to a point in the conversation and just… stop talking. She'd sit there, perfectly still, and just look at them with a pleasant expression on her face."

"Why?" Mark asked.

"Because people can't stand a vacuum," Silas said. "They're terrified of silence. They'll rush to fill it with anything. And in their rush, they often say things they never intended to. My friend learned more about a person's character in that one minute of quiet than in thirty minutes of questions."

He paused, letting the idea settle. "Another time, I was in an antique shop. Saw a piece I liked. The owner told me the price was one hundred and ninety-five dollars. I didn't say a word. I just stood there, looking at it, completely quiet. Didn't even change my expression. The man got nervous. Started talking. 'Course, that's just the sticker price,' he says. 'For you, I could do one-fifty.' My cost went down forty-five dollars without me uttering a single syllable."

An idea began to form in Mark's mind, a wild and daring strategy. "So you're saying I should just… be quiet?"

Silas paused, pushing his black plastic-frame glasses further up the bridge of his nose as if to see the situation more clearly. "I'm saying," Silas corrected gently, "that silence is golden—and a powerful tool. You don't always have to be the one talking to be in control of the conversation."

Chapter 11

Back in the office, Mark and Sarah sat in a conference room, the large monitor lit with a face from the video chat system mounted to the wall. The face introduced himself as Mr. Stone from VexTech. He was smooth, polished, and oozing with false sincerity.

"Mark, Sarah, thanks for the time," Stone began. "I've seen your engineer's notes, and I want to assure you we take quality control very, very seriously at VexTech. I think there's just been a slight misunderstanding of the performance tolerances."

For fifteen minutes, Stone tap-danced. He used jargon, quoted obscure clauses from the contract, and implied that Sarah's testing methods were flawed. It was a masterful performance of corporate deflection. Finally, he arrived at his offer.

"Look, as a gesture of our commitment to this partnership," Stone said as if doing them a great favor, "we're prepared to offer a 5% credit on your next order. And I'll personally have my team review the spec sheets again to ensure there's no confusion moving forward."

It was an insulting offer. It was nothing. Especially after the 20% offer from before. Sarah opened her mouth to argue, her face flushed with anger, but Mark laid a hand gently on her arm. She looked at him, confused.

Mark leaned back in his chair and then said nothing.

Seconds ticked by. The silence was absolute. It stretched from five seconds to ten. In the sterile conference room, it felt like an eternity. Mark could hear the faint hum of the air conditioning. He kept his breathing even, his face a neutral mask.

"Mark? Are you there?" Stone's smooth voice had a new, uncertain edge.

More silence. Mark shifted in his chair and then just waited.

"Look," Stone said, his voice faster now, the polish starting to crack. "Okay. The 5% is just an opening figure. We can… we can talk about a replacement shipment for the most recent batch, but the logistics are tricky right now…"

He trailed off. Mark remained silent. He could see Stone sweating, his carefully constructed wall of excuses crumbling into dust.

"Damn it," Stone finally spat out, the sincerity gone, replaced by raw frustration. "Listen. You want to know the real problem? My cash flow is a nightmare. I've got my own suppliers breathing down my neck. I can't afford to ship you a full replacement order on my dime and then wait ninety days for you to pay. That's why we made that great offer before. If… if you guys could pay on delivery, just for the replacement shipment, I could get you top-tier, fully tested components by the end of next week with a 10% discount. But without the cash up front, my hands are tied."

The confession hung in the silent room. Sarah stared at Mark, her eyes wide with disbelief.

Mark finally leaned forward. "Thank you for your honesty, Mr. Stone," he said, his voice calm and steady. "Let me see what I can do."

He ended the call, his heart pounding. He had the truth. But the truth had just handed him an even bigger problem: convincing his own company to prepay a supplier who had been cutting corners for months.

CHAPTER 12

The Quickest Payment

Walking to the CFO's office felt like marching toward a firing squad armed with nothing but a hopeful smile. Arthur Vance was a man made of spreadsheets and skepticism. He viewed the company's coffers not as a resource for growth, but as a hoard to be defended from the reckless optimism of every other department. He was the dragon of Innovate Dynamics, and Mark was about to ask him for a pile of gold to give to a company that had shafted them.

Mark took a deep breath and knocked on the polished mahogany door.

"Enter," a clipped voice commanded.

Arthur's office was sparse and immaculate. There were no family photos, no personal trinkets; just a desk, a computer, and a wall of financial charts. Arthur himself, a thin man with a severe haircut and wire-rimmed glasses, looked up from a ledger, his expression one of profound annoyance at being interrupted.

"Trenton. Make it quick. I'm closing out the quarter."

The Quickest Payment

Mark laid out the situation as concisely as possible: Vex-Tech's faulty components, their cash-flow problem, and the proposed solution of paying upon delivery for a single, guaranteed-quality shipment.

Arthur listened without expression, his fingers steepled. When Mark finished, he gave a short, dry laugh that was utterly devoid of humor.

"Let me see if I have this straight," he said, his voice dripping with sarcasm. "You want me to take a large sum of this company's money and give it to a vendor who has been actively selling us bad parts, based on a promise they made when you backed them into a corner? You want me to violate every sound accounting principle we have because our supplier is bad at managing their own finances?" He shook his head. "The answer is no. We don't prepay shady people. Find another vendor."

"Finding another vendor will set Project Chimera back six months, maybe more," Mark countered, keeping his voice even. "It would effectively kill the product. This is the only path forward."

"It is the most fiscally irresponsible path I have ever heard of," Arthur shot back. "The risk is unacceptable."

Mark knew a direct assault on Arthur's logic was futile. He had to change the battlefield. He had to tell a story.

"Arthur, I had a conversation with an old factory owner a while back," Mark began, leaning forward. "He told me about one of his customers, a man named Hank Berto. Back when everything was done by mail, Hank would send in a big order and include a blank, signed check. On the memo line, he'd just write, 'Not to exceed ten thousand dollars.' He did this for years."

Arthur raised an eyebrow, intrigued despite himself. "That's insane."

"That's what I thought," Mark agreed. "But this factory owner told me that no matter how big the backlog was, no matter how many other orders were ahead, Hank Berto's shipment was always the first one out the door. Always. He wasn't just a customer; he was a partner. That's the kind of loyalty that quick payment builds."

Mark let the story hang in the air for a moment before pressing his point. "This isn't about trusting VexTech. You're right, they've dropped the ball. This is a calculated risk to turn a bad supplier into a desperate, and therefore loyal, partner. We're not just buying components; we're buying their full attention. We're buying our way to the front of their line, forever."

He looked Arthur directly in the eye. "You're right to be skeptical. So here's the real question. If we don't trust them enough to make this one-time deal, why are we doing business with them at all? Because if we can't find a way to work with them, the alternative is to scrap the project. This deal, as risky as it seems, is the cheapest and fastest way to save Chimera."

Arthur was silent for a long time, his gaze fixed on Mark. The dragon was considering the argument, weighing the logic. He wasn't looking at Mark as a reckless manager anymore, but as a strategist.

"Alright, Trenton," Arthur said finally, his voice sharp as broken glass. "You've made a… plausible, if unconventional, business case." He held up a single, bony finger. "So here is my counteroffer. I will approve one— one —payment on delivery. But you, personally, will be at the loading dock when that shipment arrives. You and your engineer will inspect and sign off on every single component before my department releases one dime. If even one part is out of spec, the deal is off, VexTech is blacklisted, and you will personally explain to Richard why you flushed this money down the toilet and killed his flagship project."

He leaned back in his chair, a grim smile touching his lips. "The entire risk, Mark, is on you. Do we have a deal?"

CHAPTER 13

The Hidden Streams of Wealth

The smell of the office still clung to Mark, a faint scent of air freshener and copying machine toner. He had stared down Arthur Vance, made a daring play with VexTech, and resurrected Chimera. He had even, for a moment, seen the flicker of something akin to respect in Richard's eyes. As he drove home, the sleek, expensive sports car hugged the winding roads. The fleeting triumph felt fragile. It was built on a foundation that seemed less like solid ground, and more like a series of carefully balanced, expensive gambles. He needed to maintain his image, his reputation at Innovate Dynamics.

He pulled into the driveway, the engine's purr a stark contrast to the quiet anxiety that now filled him. He found Jen at the kitchen table, hunched over a stack of bills, a new envelope from the car dealership clutched in her hand. Her brow was furrowed, a silent testament to the stress. "Another one?" she murmured, her voice tight, nodding towards the car payment bill. "I just can't make it balance, Mark. Not with this."

He thought of the tension that had gripped their home for months, the unspoken anxieties about bills, about the future. He'd been so focused on the big, dramatic saves at work that he'd ignored the everyday leaks. When they went to bed, sleep wouldn't come. Outside he heard a constant barking. He had enough things to deal with. The sharp, repetitive sound boiled his blood and he started to imagine how he could take the dog out. In his frustration from the day and not being able to sleep, he slipped from his room. He was drawn by an instinct to the one place he knew offered quietness and clarity. He wondered if Silas would be there. Does this man ever sleep?

He found Silas on his usual bench, whittling away at a piece of wood. Mark was still hot and ripe with plans to kill the dog, "I hate my neighbor's dog and no one does anything to stop it from barking or destroying things. If they don't take care of their dog, I will!"

Silas put down his wood and knife. "Whoa, cool down," he said quietly. "You don't know what you are getting yourself into. Before illegal drugs were a problem, rural murders were usually over a woman or a dog. It's not worth starting a feud over an animal. You may be better off getting some ear plugs if you can't work it out with your neighbor because it really does turn into a mess when you can't get along with them. What's really going on?"

Mark sank onto the adjacent seat and took a deep breath. "I just can't sleep and it's got me all worked up. I'm worried about the bleeding. Even with Chimera getting back on track, I keep hearing these whispers about lost sales. It's almost like... people are just walking away from us, even when they want the product."

He paused, collecting his thoughts, a baffled expression on his face. "And it's not just the big stuff. I heard about our online store, people abandoning their carts, and I can't understand why. We offer great products, good prices. Why would they just… leave their cart? I mean, we're even being smart about inventory, making sure we don't run out. We're holding onto stock, not releasing it for sale, so we can honestly say that we are not out of stock when people order. We have to show we always have inventory, so customers don't go elsewhere. It just feels like we're losing money in ways I can't even see, like a leaky faucet, and I can't figure out what's tripping us up."

Silas chuckled, a dry rustle of leaves. "You're seeing the hidden streams now, Mark. The ones that run quietly but can still drain a well dry. As for your online store problem and folks abandoning their carts, it reminds me of a local business I saw recently. They had their check-out people answering incoming phone calls and handling returns right there at the register. Those items got priority over the customers waiting in line, and often added a considerable amount of time the paying customer must wait. I have seen people put down their intended purchases and walk out. This store's effort to save a few dollars by multitasking actually costs them. If you find abandoned items around your cash registers, you might want to question why. So, in a retail situation, streamline check-out time. Don't make your customers wait, or you'll lose them, and the money they bring. Buying needs to be quick and easy!"

The old man held up a nearly finished chess piece, a bishop with a deep, clean-cut groove in its mitered top, and examined it closely. "And that fear of selling the last one, that reminds me of a small-town tobacco shop owner from many years ago. She would not sell the last cigar in any box. She didn't want to run out of stock! It didn't make sense then - and doesn't now. She was leaving money on the table, plain as day, because of a fear that didn't serve her. Sometimes, you just gotta sell that last cigar. Don't let a misguided notion of scarcity stop you from making the sale. Every item bought, every service rendered, keeps the flow going. Whenever you sell something, you have money to make more money."

Mark listened, the practical wisdom sinking in. He felt a familiar comfort in Silas's presence, the quiet understanding that allowed him to drop his guard. He took a deep breath, and the deeper, more personal anxieties began to spill out. "It's not just the company, Silas. It's... it's at home too. The bills. Jen and I are arguing. We've got this new car, and it's just..." He trailed off, gesturing vaguely, the unspoken weight of the car payment looming. "I thought I needed it for work, for my image. To show I'm on top of things, you know? But it's just making everything so tight. Jen's trying to balance the books, and it just doesn't balance."

Silas paused, making a delicate cut on his carving. "I remember a young couple, Frank and Mary. Started out so happy, but Frank always had to have the newest, shiniest thing. A bigger TV, a faster boat, then a luxury car like yours. Mary kept trying to balance the books, asking him to slow down, but he always said he 'needed' these things. The tension, it just built up, like water behind a dam. Eventually, the dam broke. All that stress, all those arguments over bills, just slowly eroded everything they had. The marriage couldn't survive being constantly underwater. They ended up losing more than just money. They lost each other. When you're not living paycheck to paycheck and you've got that buffer, it opens doors, Mark. It's not about being cheap, it's about being free. That's how you live below your means – not because you're poor, but because you're wise."

Mark nodded slowly, the pieces clicking into place. He had been so focused on the big, dramatic saves that he'd overlooked the fundamental importance of these smaller, consistent principles. They were the silent architects of financial strength, both personally and for Innovate Dynamics.

Mark headed home with lots to think about. It was getting late, and he knew he needed the sleep, but still sitting at the back of his mind were those parts from VexTech. Would they work or would they sink all his efforts?

CHAPTER 14

The Extra Casting

The air on the loading dock was cold and smelled of diesel fumes and damp concrete. Mark's career felt as fragile as the morning mist burning off the asphalt. He stood beside Sarah, both of them clad in bright yellow safety vests, watching the bay door rumble open. Arthur Vance's words echoed in his ears: "The entire risk, Mark, is on you."

A large VexTech truck backed slowly into the bay, its air brakes hissing like a nest of snakes. The driver hopped out, clipboard in hand, and opened the rear doors with a metallic clang. Inside, stacked neatly on pallets, were dozens of boxes containing the precious micro-controllers—the components that could save Project Chimera or end Mark's career at Innovate Dynamics.

For the next two hours, Mark and Sarah worked with a focused intensity. They opened box after box, pulling random samples while the nervous truck driver looked on. Sarah set up a portable testing station on a fold-out table, her fingers flying across the diagnostic equipment. Mark's job was to ferry the components, his stomach twisting into a tighter knot with every sample she tested.

He watched her face, looking for any flicker of disappointment, any sign of failure. But there was none.

"They're good, Mark," she said finally, looking up from her equipment with a tired but triumphant smile. "They're all good. Every single one is hitting 1.2 gigahertz, no problem. These are the parts they promised us."

A wave of relief so powerful it made him dizzy, washed over Mark. He pulled out his phone, sent a one-word text to Arthur Vance— "Approved" —and watched as the forklift operators began to unload the shipment that would bring Chimera back to life. He had won. He had stared down the dragon and walked out of the fire unscathed.

Later that day, the victory felt strangely hollow. He had navigated a series of professional minefields, but he felt a pull back to the park, back to the bench by the pond. He needed to understand the why behind his success, not just the what.

He found Silas there, as always. Mark sat down next to him and began recounting the series of events: the tense phone call, the high-stakes negotiation with Arthur, the triumphant inspection on the loading dock.

Silas listened, a small smile playing on his lips. "You did good, Mark. You're learning to use the right tools for the job." He held up the half-finished chess piece in his hand—a tall, stately king, awaiting its finishing cross. "But you're still thinking about it like a fight. Like you won. Sometimes, the goal isn't to win, but to understand."

He set the king down. "My old mentor, Cal Fletcher, the man I bought the factory from, he was a master of understanding people. When I was a young man, just a supervisor

The Extra Casting

on the floor, he decided to test me. One of the machines we packed had a heavy, four-pound iron casting that had to be removed and packed separately in the box. One afternoon, as I was finishing up a pallet, I noticed an extra casting sitting on the packing bench."

Mark listened intently, picturing the scene.

"My first thought," Silas continued, "was that I must have forgotten to put one in a box. The old way to fix that was to start ripping open boxes until you found the empty one. A waste of time and material. But I stopped and thought. I went and got the shipping scale, and I started weighing each box. The one that was four pounds lighter would be the one missing the part."

Silas's eyes twinkled behind his thick, black glasses at the memory. "Cal had been watching from his office. He walked out onto the floor. 'You don't have to do that, son,' he said. I told him I'd messed up and left a casting out. And he smiled and told me he had put the extra one there on purpose, just to see what I would do. He said everyone else before me had always started ripping open the boxes."

The story settled on Mark, but the meaning was different this time.

"He wasn't testing you to see if you would fail," Mark said slowly, the pieces clicking into place.

"Exactly!" Silas beamed. "He wasn't looking for my weakness. He was looking for my strength. He wanted to see if I could find a better way. And because he did that, I spent the rest of my career trying to do the same for my people. It's okay to test your people, but you should be looking for their strengths, not their weaknesses."

The simple wisdom shined light in a dark spot in Mark's mind, but it wasn't his professional life that flashed before his eyes. It was a memory from two nights ago. His son, Colton, had been struggling with his math homework, his textbook a mess of frustrated scribbles. Mark had stood over him, his patience wearing thin. "It's not that hard, Colton! Just focus! You're not even trying!"

He saw his son's face crumple. He saw the way Colton had pushed the math book away and retreated into the world of his sketchbook, a world filled with fantastical creatures and intricate landscapes that Mark had always dismissed as a distraction.

He had been testing his son. Every single day. But he hadn't been looking for Colton's strengths. He had only been looking for his weaknesses, pointing them out, and demanding he fix them.

The victory on the loading dock suddenly felt like ashes in his mouth. He had spent the week becoming a better manager, but he was failing at the only job that truly mattered.

CHAPTER 15

The Crucible of Command

The first alarm blared from Mark's phone at 2:17 AM, a piercing, digital scream that ripped him from a dead sleep. It was a system-wide, code-red alert from the network operations center. Before he could even sit up, a second alarm, and then a third, joined the chorus. He grabbed his phone. The screen was a cascade of automated warnings: "SERVER FAILURE: ATL-01," "NETWORK OFFLINE: MAJOR CLIENTS," "CASCADE ERROR: AUTHENTICATION FAILURE."

The office was a scene of controlled chaos. A handful of bleary-eyed engineers were huddled around a bank of monitors, their faces illuminated by the frantic scroll of error logs. At the center of it all was Sarah, her expression grim, a phone pressed to each ear.

"No, I don't have an ETA!" she barked into one phone, while typing furiously with one hand. "The whole array is down."

The old Mark would have dived right into the technical details, adding to the noise, demanding answers, getting in the way. But he remembered how Silas had told him about what happened during a government crisis. A key official started helping people evacuate after a large explosion at their headquarters and he couldn't be found. While it may have been honorable, he was one of the few who had the authority to make critical atomic decisions. When he got caught up in the details, he missed the big picture. Mark remembered the lesson: In an emergency situation, take a mental step back and away. Look around at what is being done and what is NOT being taken care of.

He stood back from the huddle, his eyes scanning the room. The engineers were focused on the technical problem. That was being handled. But what wasn't being handled? The phones were ringing off the hook with calls from their panicked clients. The junior IT staff were running around like headless chickens, with no clear direction. No one was governing the flow of information. No one was leading. The supervisors were all working so hard they had forgotten to manage.

"Sarah," he said, his voice cutting through the din. She looked up, her eyes wide with stress. "What is the one thing you need right now to solve this?"

"I need to find the point of failure," she said, "but I'm drowning in redundant alerts and client calls."

"Okay," Mark said, his mind clicking into place. He turned to the junior staff. "You two, you're on the phone. Your only job is to tell our clients that we have an outage, our top people are on it, and we will call them back the second we have an update. Be calm, be professional. No speculation." He pointed to another. "You, get a pot of coffee going. A big one."

He turned back to Sarah. "I'm running interference. No one stops you but me. You have one job: find the problem." He had just delegated the most critical task to his subordinate. He felt a pang of fear, the urge to micromanage, but he pushed it down. He had to trust her. When you put a subordinate in a position requiring him to make a decision, go with that decision.

An hour later, Sarah had already concluded it wasn't a hardware failure or a malicious attack. So she had enlisted Clark Daniels and they were reviewing the server code. Clark was their veteran software engineer. He had more gray hair growing out of his ears than from the top of his head.

"It's in the core architecture," Clark said, his voice tight with a mixture of anger and disbelief. He pointed to a section of code on her screen. "The new load-balancing protocol. It's elegant, creative, innovative… and fatally flawed. It doesn't account for real-world network latency under stress. It's creating a feedback loop that's corrupting data packets across the entire array." Sarah's fingers flew across the keyboard, bringing up a new window on the screen. "I'm checking the commit history for this module. Who wrote this?" The log appeared, and she pointed to the top entry. "There it is. It's the code we just pushed to production. I knew it. Kevin Tanaka."

The name exploded across the room like a grenade. Kevin Tanaka. Mark's memory flashed instantly to the young man who was rarely seen without his noise-canceling headphones. With his messy hair, they joked that he never took a shower. He had a regular, quiet smirk that suggested he was operating on a higher intellectual plane than everyone else in the room. He was a prodigy on paper, armed with a freshly minted master's from a prestigious university and a portfolio of theoretical projects that were as dazzling as they were impractical. He treated Clark like a relic, dismissing his time-tested protocols as 'inelegant' and his warnings as the ramblings of the obsolete. Mark remembered signing off on this very project, swayed by the slick presentation and ignoring the quiet concerns of his senior staff.

Mark had to make a choice, and he had to make it now. They could try to patch Kevin's flawed code on the fly—a risky, complex procedure that could make things even worse. Or they could do the unthinkable: take the entire system offline, roll back the code, and restore a safe data backup, a process that would be faster and more certain, but could result in the loss of a full day's worth of client data. It was a terrible choice.

He looked at Sarah, at the exhausted faces of the engineers. There was no time to waver. As Silas had said to him once, " When you need to make a decision - make it."

"Take it all offline," Mark said, his voice ringing with an authority he didn't know he possessed. "Shut it down. We'll roll it back and restore from the backups. I'll handle the clients."

He spent the rest of the night on the phone, personally calling the CEO of every affected client, explaining the situation, the data loss, and the recovery plan. It was the hardest thing he had ever had to do.

As the sun rose, casting a gray, exhausted light into the office, the system flickered back to life. The crisis was over. They had survived. But as Mark looked at the tired, drained faces of his team, he knew the victory was a brutal one. He had been through the crucible, and the experience had burned away the last of his naivete about what it truly meant to lead.

Mark stared at the restored, stable network—running on the old, reliable protocols Kevin had dismissed. He thought of Clark, of the quiet competence that came from decades of real-world problem-solving. It wasn't just about the time Clark had put in; it was about the growth. Mark realized that an employee can have 20 years of experience, or they can have one year's experience 20 times. Clark was the former, a man whose expertise had deepened with every challenge. Mark had seen too many of the latter in his career—people who mistake repetition for experience. Kevin, on the other hand, was at the beginning of his journey and Mark wondered where he would end up in 20 years. Right now Kevin was clever and intelligent with his flashy degree. It wasn't the knowledge from the degree that was the problem; it was the arrogance that came with it, the ignorance of not knowing what you don't know. That's when Mark came to the conclusion: the most dangerous thing in the world is a brand-new engineering degree.

CHAPTER 16

Growing Like Flowers

The guilt was a weight, heavier than any project deadline or supply chain crisis. It sat on his chest as he drove home after an extra-long day, making each breath feel shallow. The image of Colton's crestfallen face was burned into his mind. He was so busy learning to be a better leader to his employees that he had forgotten how to be a father to his own son.

He walked into a house thick with a familiar, tense silence. Jen was at the kitchen counter, sorting through a stack of mail, her back rigid. Colton was nowhere to be seen.

"Hey," Mark said, his voice quiet.

"Hey," Jen replied, not looking up. The single word was loaded with a week's worth of frustration.

He found Colton in his room, not drawing, but staring blankly at the same hated math textbook from the other night. The sketchbook lay closed on his bed.

"How's it going, buddy?" Mark asked, trying to sound casual.

Colton just shrugged, his shoulders slumping.

Mark sat on the edge of the bed, his mind racing. He wanted to apologize, to fix it, but the words felt clumsy and inadequate. He looked at his son, at the way his brow was furrowed in concentration. Looking at Colton's face, Mark was struck by how much older he seemed. Then a memory from Silas came to Mark's mind. Mark had told Silas his kid was "growing like a weed," and Silas had gently corrected him. "No," the old man had said. "He is growing like a flower."

Mark had thought it was a charming little anecdote at the time. Now, looking at his son, he understood the profound truth behind it. Weeds were a nuisance, a problem to be dealt with. Flowers were something to be nurtured, admired for their unique beauty, and given what they needed to bloom. He had been treating his son like a weed.

"You know, you're getting really tall," Mark said, the words coming out softer than he intended. Mark chuckled to himself. He'd never liked the common phrase, 'you're getting big.' Was that really a compliment? 'Getting tall,' however, felt like a true measure of growth.

Colton looked up, a flicker of surprise in his eleven-year-old eyes. "I am?"

"Yeah," Mark said, a real smile touching his lips for the first time that evening. You are probably about as tall as your Mom. A small, shy smile crept onto Colton's face. It was a start. A tiny seed planted in barren ground.

Later that night, after Colton was in bed, the silence between Mark and Jen returned, heavier than before. She was wiping down the already spotless kitchen counters, her movements sharp and angry.

"We can't keep doing this, Mark," she said finally, her voice tight with unshed tears. "You're a ghost in this house. You're here, but you're not. Colton feels it. I feel it. It's like all your focus, all your energy, is for that place. There's nothing left for us."

"I know," he said, the two words costing him a mountain of pride. "I've been… I've been getting it wrong."

"You've been getting it wrong for years," she corrected, her voice breaking. "I love you, Mark, but I'm so tired. I feel like I'm holding this family together by myself, and my hands are getting scraped raw."

The raw pain in her voice was a knife in his gut. He wanted to promise her he would change, that he would fix everything, but he knew it was a promise he had made and broken a dozen times before.

The next evening, he found himself back at the park. The sun was setting, and the air was cool. He told Silas everything, his voice thick with shame as he recounted the scene with Colton and the raw, painful conversation with Jen.

"I feel like I'm failing at everything that matters," Mark confessed, his voice barely a whisper.

Silas was quiet for a long time, whittling a piece of wood, the shape of a queen was emerging as pieces of wood fell before him. "You're not failing, Mark," he said finally. "You're just learning what the real prize is."

He looked up from his work, his eyes holding a deep, sad wisdom. "Let me tell you something I learned a long, long time ago. Whatever you want most in life, you will never attain to your satisfaction. If it's money, you'll never feel rich enough. If it's fame, you'll never be famous enough. You'll spend your whole life chasing a horizon that keeps moving away from you."

He paused, his gaze steady. "But if your wife's love is your keenest desire, you'll spend every day trying to be a man who is worthy of it. And the results of that are pretty good."

Silas looked out over the pond. "My Eleanor and I… we went through some hard times. Real hard times. Lost our little girl. Scraped by on nothing for years. You know what we talked about when we got old? Not the good times when money was easy. We talked about the winters we survived on canned vegetables from her mother's garden. We talked about the nights we held each other and cried until we had nothing left. We smiled about those times. You have to cherish the hard times, Mark. They're the fire that forges a bond that can't be broken."

Silas went on, "Mark, this is hard to say, and if you are willing to receive it, it will change everything. God is crafting a story in your life, and when things get hard for you, He is bringing you to the end of yourself. We all have to come to this place if we want to see His power at work in our lives. We often pursue doing things where we are in control, but it is not till we can rest in Him that we see God move in power. Paul in the Bible said that God's power was made perfect in his weakness. God is bringing you through these challenges to craft a testimony worth telling."

He turned back to Mark, his expression serious. "You're worried about money and providing. That's honorable. But remember how I said you should live below your means. Debt is a four-letter word. The stress of money will poison everything if you let it. The security you're trying to build for your family isn't in your bank account. It's in your presence. It's in their hearts. When you pursue the right things in life, God will provide for you."

Mark sat in the deepening twilight, the weight of Silas's words settling over him. He had been chasing the horizon, trying to build a fortress of success, while the real treasure was in a house just a few miles away, waiting for him to simply come home.

CHAPTER 17

A Project Without a Champion

The new VexTech components worked like a charm. With the right parts, Sarah's team assembled the Chimera prototypes in record time. The project, once on life support, was suddenly breathing on its own. Mark's status at the office solidified from 'competent manager' to 'miracle worker.' But with the operational crisis averted, Richard's attention snapped back to his original plan.

"The product is viable, which is great," Richard announced in a leadership meeting, beaming as if he'd personally soldered every circuit board. "Now we need to make a splash. David, your marketing blitz. It's back on. Full budget. I want to see Innovate Dynamics everywhere."

David preened, shooting a triumphant smirk across the table at Mark. "My team is ready to deploy, Richard. Project 'Apex Predator' is a go."

Over the next week, Mark watched from a distance as Project Apex Predator took shape. David was in his element, holding court in flashy presentations filled with buzzwords and stock photos of smiling, diverse millennials. He talked about "synergizing brand momentum" and "disrupting the vertical." It was a performance, and David was its star.

But as Mark observed, a deep sense of unease began to grow. He saw the way David interacted with his team. He never asked questions; he only gave orders. He was dismissive of the graphic designers' concerns about the tight deadlines and waved away the copywriters' questions about the target audience. The entire project was an extension of his own ego. He wasn't in the trenches with his people; he was on a balcony, preparing to take a bow.

Mark was walking past a conference room when he overheard Chloe, one of the designers, talking to a colleague. "I don't get it," she was saying, sounding exhausted. "He wants the ads to scream 'speed and affordability,' but our own report said our advantage is in reliability and customer service. It feels like we're ignoring our own research."

The comment confirmed Mark's growing unease. He thought of Silas, of the stories he told, of the simple truths that underpinned them. He realized he was witnessing a fundamental law of leadership in action: If the person overseeing a project is not on board with it, the project has a low chance of success. David wasn't truly on board with the project's success; he was on board with the appearance of success. He didn't care about the details, the research, or the people doing the work. He only cared about the launch party.

A Project Without a Champion

The old Mark would have seen this as an opportunity to watch his rival fail. He could have sat back, collected evidence of the impending disaster, and said, "I told you so." But that was the old game, the zero-sum game of office politics. Silas's wisdom had shown him a different path. His long-term goal wasn't to beat David; it was to help Innovate Dynamics succeed.

He didn't go to Richard. He didn't confront David. Instead, he took a different approach. He found Chloe in the breakroom later that day.

"I overheard what you said earlier," he told her quietly. "About the messaging. You're right."

Chloe looked up, startled and a little scared, as if she'd been caught criticizing the king.

"Your instincts are spot on," Mark continued. "You and your team are the ones doing the real work. What do you need?"

It was a simple question, but for Chloe, it was revolutionary. No one in management had ever asked her that before. Hesitantly at first, and then with growing confidence, she explained the team's frustrations, their ideas, and the better, more effective campaign they knew they could build if anyone would just listen.

Mark didn't offer solutions. He just listened, asked questions, and made sure she had access to all the data from the Apex report. He was playing the long game. He wasn't trying to save David's failing project. He was supporting the people who would be there to build the next one.

Chapter 17

A few days later, David proudly circulated the first proofs of the "Apex Predator" ad campaign. The headline, in a bold, aggressive font, screamed: "Innovate Dynamics: Cheaper. Faster. Better."

Mark stared at it, a cold knot forming in his stomach. It was a lie, printed in full color. They weren't cheaper. With the VexTech components, they were significantly more expensive. And they weren't faster. Their strength was in their durability and support. The ad was a beautiful, expensive, and utterly false promise. It was a train wreck in the making, and it was accelerating right toward them.

CHAPTER 18

The Other Man's Game

The news broke not with a bang, but with a ping. A news alert on Mark's phone from a major financial publication. The headline made him sick: "Activist Investor Stratton Corp Acquires 8% Stake in Innovate Dynamics, Signals Intent for Hostile Takeover."

A wave of cold dread washed over Mark, colder and sharper than any he had felt before. He knew the name. Everyone in the industry knew Stratton Corp. They were corporate vultures, famous for buying struggling companies, gutting them for parts, laying off thousands, and selling the hollowed-out shell for a profit. They weren't builders; they were demolition experts.

Within minutes, the office was a hive of panicked energy. Whispers turned into anxious chatter. Mark saw people secretively updating their resumes on their screens. The air, which had just started to feel hopeful, was now thick with the metallic taste of fear. This wasn't a competitor like Apex; this was an executioner.

Chapter 18

Richard called an emergency leadership meeting. The mood in the room was grim.

"They're coming for us," Richard said, his face pale. "Stratton's playbook is always the same. They'll tear us apart. We have to fight back. We have to show the board we're tough, that we're lean. That we can be just as ruthless as they are."

David, smelling blood in the water, saw his opportunity. "Richard's right. This is a street fight. We need to get ahead of them. Announce a proactive restructuring. Immediate 15% headcount reduction across the board. Freeze all R&D spending. We show the board we can make the hard cuts ourselves. We'll look strong, decisive."

Mark listened in horror. David's plan was to save the company by killing it. They would be destroying their greatest assets—their people, their culture of innovation—just to look tough. They would be burning down their own house to keep the wolves from the door.

He thought of Silas, of a conversation they'd had weeks ago while sitting by the pond. Silas had been telling him about a rival factory that had tried to copy his every move, from his products to his marketing. "They were always one step behind," Silas had said with a chuckle. "Never understood that if you play the other man's game, you will always lose. You can't beat someone at a game they invented. You have to play your own."

The memory was a lifeline in a sea of panic.

"No," Mark said, his voice cutting through the fearful consensus. Every head in the room turned to him.

"No?" Richard repeated, his voice dangerously low.

"We can't play their game," Mark said, standing up, his hands flat on the conference table. "Stratton Corp is the best in the world at one thing: butchering companies. If we try to be ruthless, we'll just be a bad imitation. We'll lose. We have to play our game."

"And what game is that, Mark?" David sneered. "The one where we all hold hands and sing Kumbaya while they sell our office furniture?"

Mark ignored him, his eyes locked on Richard. "Our game is building things. Our strength is our people—people like Sarah and Chloe and their teams. Our advantage is the loyalty we build with our customers, and the reliability of our products. That's what we should be showcasing, not destroying."

He took a breath, remembering a story a trusted friend had told him. "A friend of mine once told me about a company called Charter Carburetor. They thought they were in the business of building carburetors. But when fuel injection came along, they went out of business. They got it wrong. They weren't in the carburetor business; they were in the fuel delivery business. They didn't define their purpose correctly, and it killed them."

He looked around the table at the stunned faces. "We have to ask ourselves the same question. What business are we really in? Are we in the business of making cheap tech widgets? Because if we are, Stratton is right, and we're already dead. Or are we in the business of providing reliable, long-term tech solutions with unparalleled human support? Because if that's our business, then laying off the very people who provide that support is insane. It's corporate suicide."

He had laid all his cards on the table. He was betting everything on a principle, on a piece of wisdom from an old man in a park.

Richard stared at him, his face an unreadable mask. The silence stretched, thick and heavy. Mark's heart pounded in his chest. He had either just saved the soul of the company, or he had just talked himself out of a job.

CHAPTER 19

The Drama of the Glasses

The silence in the conference room was a tangible thing, a heavy blanket smothering all sound. Mark could feel every eye on him. David's gaze was pure venom. Richard's was something else entirely—shock, anger, and a flicker of something Mark couldn't name.

"Get out," Richard said, his voice a low growl. "All of you. Except Mark."

The room emptied in a hurried, silent shuffle. When the door clicked shut, Richard sank into his chair, rubbing his temples.

"You've got a hell of a nerve, Trenton," he said, his voice weary. "Contradicting me in front of the entire leadership team. You think I don't know what Stratton will do to us?"

"I think you do," Mark said quietly. "And I think you're a builder, not a butcher. You built this company. David's plan is to burn it down to collect the insurance money."

Richard was silent for a long moment. "You've got twenty-four hours," he said finally, looking up, his eyes hard. "You bring me a real plan. A plan to fight our way, not their way. If I like it, we do it. If I don't... You can clean out your desk. David's marketing campaign is officially dead. Now get out of my office."

The news of the campaign's cancellation spread through the office like wildfire. David was publicly humiliated, his authority shattered. And he knew exactly who to blame.

Mark was heading to the breakroom for a much-needed coffee when David cornered him in the hallway. A small crowd of employees, sensing drama, began to slow their pace, pretending to check their phones.

"There you are," David said, his voice loud enough to carry. "I've been looking for you. The photographer for the Apex Predator shoot just walked out. Said he couldn't do the shoot because your department failed to deliver the final Chimera prototype. My entire launch is being sabotaged by your incompetence!"

It was a petty, transparent lie. The prototype had been delivered to marketing two days ago. But David wasn't interested in the truth. He was interested in a public execution.

Mark felt a surge of adrenaline. He could argue. He could pull up the delivery logs on his phone and prove David was a liar. But he saw the trap. Arguing would just be slinging mud. It would be a messy, public spectacle that would make them both look bad and solve nothing. He needed to end the confrontation, not win it. He needed a circuit breaker. An idea, born of desperation and a flash of theatrical inspiration, exploded in his mind. It was crazy. It was a risk. But it was better than wrestling in the mud.

The Drama of the Glasses

He reached into his shirt pocket and pulled out his only pair of glasses. As David opened his mouth to launch another volley of accusations, Mark acted.

He held the glasses up in front of him, twisted them in his hands with a sharp CRACK of plastic, and hurled the two pieces against the far wall of the hallway.

"I'VE HAD ENOUGH OF THIS!" he roared, his voice echoing in the sudden, shocked silence. The echo died, leaving only the sound of a plastic lens rolling across the floor.

Every person in the hallway froze. David's mouth hung open, his attack forgotten. The crowd of onlookers stared, wide-eyed.

Mark didn't say another word. He turned and walked back to his office, his heart hammering against his ribs. He glanced back. The crowd was already dispersing, whispering excitedly. David was still standing there, his face a mask of stunned disbelief, completely disarmed. Mark had ended the battle without throwing a single punch.

A couple of minutes later, when everyone was gone, he saw Jack sweeping up the last of the plastic shards from his earlier performance. The janitor worked with a quiet focus, not looking up until Mark was right beside him.

"Sometimes," Jack said, tapping the last of the debris into his dustpan, "you gotta break something small to fix something big." He gave Mark a quick, knowing glance and then continued on his way, a black pair of glasses bouncing in and out of his back pocket as he walked. He left Mark standing alone in the hallway. The staff understood, David was just being a jerk, and people weren't putting up with it anymore.

Sure enough, as the day progressed, David dropped the matter and stayed in his office the rest of the day.

On his way home that day, Mark stopped at the discount store and bought another pair of reading glasses for a dollar plus tax. As he walked out, he couldn't help but smile, thinking it was one of the best dollars he had ever spent.

CHAPTER 20

The Anchor at Home

Mark came home that night feeling like a stranger in his own life. The confrontation with David, the impossible 24-hour deadline from Richard—it all felt like a movie he was watching from a great distance. The only thing that felt real was the exhaustion, a bone-deep weariness that had nothing to do with being tired.

He found Jen in the living room, curled on the sofa with a book, a cup of tea steaming on the end table. The house was quiet. The air was peaceful. It felt like a different universe from the one he had just left.

"Tough day?" she asked, her voice soft. She didn't sound accusatory, just observant.

He sank onto the other end of the sofa, the space between them feeling like a canyon. "You have no idea."

He didn't intend to tell her everything, but it all came spilling out—the takeover threat, David's plan to gut the company, his own desperate stand in the boardroom, the absurd, theatrical drama with the glasses. He told her about the 24-hour deadline hanging over his head.

When he finished, he expected judgment, or maybe just a tired sigh. Instead, she looked at him with a new kind of understanding.

"I've been watching you, Mark," she said. "This last month. You're changing. You're… calmer. Even with all this chaos."

"I don't feel calm," he admitted. "I feel like I'm walking on a tightrope. I even broke my glasses."

"But you weren't out of control when you broke them, and you're walking the tightrope," she said. "Before, you would have just worked harder, stayed later, tried to manage every little detail until you collapsed. You're not doing that now. You're thinking differently."

He thought of Silas, of the endless stream of stories and simple truths. "I've been getting some advice from a friend," he said. "An old-timer. He's helped me see things." He looked at her, needing her to understand. "He told me that for years, I've been acting like a driver, just wrestling with the steering wheel. He said I needed to become an operator, someone so in tune with the machine that it just responds. That's what I'm trying to do. At work, and…" he trailed off, looking around the quiet room, "here."

She let out a deep breath, "I knew you were going somewhere and followed you one night when Colton was at a sleepover. When I saw the old man, I at least knew you weren't having an affair. I guessed he was helping you since I could tell things were improving."

Mark admitted it was pretty weird going to a park at all hours, but Silas somehow was always there when he needed him. Mark broke down as he was so grateful for his help and that he was finally feeling connected with his wife. Then he confessed to her how he had been working against her, not with her, like the gruff building inspector who talks down to people while working. He told her how he realized his focus on Colton's grades was like only looking for what was wrong, instead of celebrating what was right.

"Remember when I said Colton was growing like a flower?" he asked. "That came from him, too. It's one of those little things, a simple catchphrase, but it changed everything for me. It made me realize that my employees—and my family—will focus on what they believe is important to me. And for too long, I've been showing them that the only thing that mattered was the crisis of the day."

Jen's eyes were glistening. She set her book aside and moved closer to him on the sofa.

"I'm sorry, Jen," he said, his voice thick with emotion. "I know I've been a driver in this family, not an operator. I've been so busy trying to solve all the problems that I forgot to just be here." He managed a small, tired smile. "My friend even had a piece of advice for that. He said, 'Don't solve all the problems in your business. Save a couple of small ones. If your employees don't have something to complain about, they may invent a large problem.' Maybe that's what we need. A few small, unimportant problems to solve together."

She laughed, a real, beautiful laugh that he hadn't heard in months. She reached out and took his hand.

"I don't need you to solve all the problems, Mark," she said, her thumb tracing circles on the back of his hand. "I just need you here, with me, to face them." She was feeling the bond growing that people call, "love".

He squeezed her hand, feeling a profound sense of peace settle over him. His wife seemed to respect him more for his honesty. The storm was still raging at work. The deadline was still looming. But for the first time, he felt a solid foundation beneath his feet. The strategies and truth weren't just in the wisdom of an old man in a park. It was here, in this room, in the warmth of his wife's hand.

CHAPTER 21

The Final Presentation

The boardroom felt like a courtroom where the verdict had already been decided. The air was stale and heavy with the scent of expensive wood polish and quiet panic. Seated around the long, intimidating table were the members of Innovate Dynamics' board, their faces grim. At the head of the table sat Richard. To his right sat a woman Mark didn't recognize—impeccably dressed, with sharp, intelligent eyes that missed nothing. She was Catherine Sterling, the managing partner of a private equity firm, their potential "white knight" investor. She was their only hope. Across from her, looking sullen and defeated, was David.

Richard had given Mark twenty-four hours. Mark had used every second. He hadn't built a PowerPoint deck full of charts and projections. He had built a story.

"The floor is yours, Mark," Richard said, his voice flat.

Mark walked to the front of the room, leaving his laptop on the table. He felt a strange calm settle over him. He had nothing to lose. He had already faced down his own failures at work and home. This was just a conversation.

"Good morning," he began, his voice steady. "A few months ago, this company was on the verge of collapse. Project Chimera was failing, our suppliers were unreliable, and our competitors were eating us alive. We were losing. And a lot of that was my fault."

He let the admission hang in the air, a shocking moment of public accountability. He could feel David's smug gaze, see the flicker of surprise on the board members' faces. This was the first principle of his new strategy: Effective leaders share the credit, but they shoulder the blame.

"I was so focused on managing the crisis," Mark continued, "that I forgot to lead the people. I was looking at spreadsheets instead of talking to the engineers. I was trying to solve problems I didn't even understand."

He then told them a story. Not a corporate fable, but the real, unvarnished story of the last few months. He told them about Sarah Jenkins, the brilliant engineer who was fighting a battle no one could see. He told them about the faulty components from VexTech. He put the numbers on the screen—not projections, but hard data. The failure rates of the old components versus the perfect performance of the new ones. The cost of the delays. The price of not listening.

Then, he did something no one expected.

"But I can't tell this part of the story as well as she can," he said. "Sarah, could you join me for a moment?"

A stunned Sarah Jenkins, whom Mark had asked to be on standby just outside the room, walked in. For five minutes, in her own words, she explained the technical turnaround.

The Final Presentation

She spoke with a passion and clarity that no manager could replicate. Mark saw the board members lean in, captivated. He saw Catherine Sterling make a note on her pad.

He then brought up the data from his Apex report, showing the numbers that proved their competitor's weakness was in customer support. "We have campaigned that we were cheaper and faster," Mark explained, not with malice, but as a statement of fact. "But the numbers show that isn't our strength. It isn't our game. Our game is reliability. Our game is trust."

He then called on Chloe, the designer from David's own team. Visibly nervous, but gaining confidence under Mark's reassuring gaze, Chloe presented a mock-up of a new marketing campaign—one her team had developed in secret. The slogan wasn't aggressive. It was a simple, powerful promise: "Innovate Dynamics: Built to Last. Here to Help." Then, under it, in small, clean letters, it had their story: "Achieve excellent quality control and eliminate returns with our reliable automated technology for manufacturers." It was honest. It was real. It was clear who their audience was and told them how they could solve their problems.

As Chloe finished to a stunned silence, Mark stepped forward to conclude. "Stratton Corp wants you to believe this company is a collection of assets to be stripped and sold. They are wrong. This company is a collection of people. Smart, dedicated people. We have considered the strategy to fight a fast, chaotic war. My strategy is to win by embracing a regular, steady pace. We will win by making our products better, one component at a time. By improving our customer service, one call at a time. By building a culture of trust, one person at a time."

He looked directly at Catherine Sterling. "That is our plan. We will not be the cheapest or the flashiest. We will be the company you can count on. We will be the anchor in the storm."

He finished. The silence that followed was absolute. He had shared the credit, told a story, used numbers, and shouldered the blame. He had laid out a vision based on every piece of wisdom he had gathered.

Catherine Sterling tapped her pen on her notepad. She looked at Richard, then at the board, and then her sharp, intelligent eyes settled on Mark.

"Mr. Trenton," she said, her voice cool and precise. "That was a very compelling story. But you've based your entire strategy on turning this company into a premium, service-oriented brand." She leaned forward slightly. "Tell me, how do you plan to do that when your own marketing department just spent the last few months trying to convince the world you were a discount bargain bin?"

CHAPTER 22

The Anchor Holds

Catherine Sterling's question was a dagger, sharp and perfectly aimed. It cut through the hopeful atmosphere Mark had built, exposing the one glaring weakness in his entire plan: the damage was already done. He could feel David's smirk without even looking at him. This was the killing blow.

Mark met her gaze. He didn't have a clever answer. He didn't have a chart or a projection. All he had was the truth.

"You're right," he said, his voice quiet but firm. "We did. And it was a mistake. It was a mistake because we weren't being honest about who we are. Rebuilding that trust won't be fast, and it won't be easy. It starts today, with honesty. It continues by us doing exactly what we say we're going to do. We won't win back our reputation with a flashy ad campaign. We'll win it back one customer, one successful installation, one positive service call at a time. It's slow. It's methodical. But it's real."

He paused, a final piece of Silas's wisdom clicking into place. "We only win at the things we focus on. For the last six months, we've been focused on the wrong things: on our competitors, on our image, on our own internal fears. Starting today, we are going to focus on one thing and one thing only: our customers' success. Our most valuable clients are the ones we already have and by helping them succeed we will keep them coming back and attract new ones too. If we do that, everything else will follow."

Catherine Sterling held his gaze for a long, unblinking moment. Then, a slow smile spread across her face. She closed her notepad, the sound echoing in the silent room.

"Gentlemen," she said, addressing the board but still looking at Mark. "I believe I've seen enough. My firm is prepared to make a significant investment in Innovate Dynamics. On one condition." She turned to Richard. "Mr. Trenton is put in charge of the Chimera product launch. All of it. From operations to marketing. End to end."

The relief in the room was nearly audible as those gathered let out the breath they had seemed to be holding since they entered the room. The board members, who had been sitting like statues, were now visibly relaxed. Richard nodded, a look of profound relief on his face. "Done."

The meeting adjourned. As the board members stood up, shaking Mark's hand, he felt a strange sense of detachment. There was no surge of adrenaline, no thrill of victory. Just a quiet, deep-seated peace.

He saw Sarah and Chloe hovering nervously by the door. He walked right past the congratulating board members and went straight to them.

"We did it," he said, a genuine smile on his face. He looked at Richard and the board members, who were watching them. "These are the two people who saved this company today. Not me."

He turned back to them, his voice full of a warmth they had never heard from him before. "Call your families. Tell them the good news. Tell them you're the heroes today. They deserve to hear it."

He watched as they pulled out their phones, their faces glowing. He had learned that it wasn't enough to praise people in private. When you award or praise an employee, you have to make sure the spouse and family see it, too.

Later, there was an impromptu celebration in the main conference room. Someone had gotten coffee orders from a local coffee shop and brought a bunch of donuts. People were laughing, clapping him on the back. But Mark's mind was elsewhere. He was thinking about how he had helped Sarah find her voice, how he had empowered Chloe to trust her instincts. He was realizing that his duty wasn't just to manage people, but to help them grow. As a leader, it is your duty to help your people improve themselves.

He slipped out of the celebration unnoticed. The victory felt good, but it didn't feel like the end of the journey. It felt like the beginning. He walked out of the office, not toward the park, but toward his car. He knew where he needed to go. He had another team to lead, another person to build up. He had to get home.

CHAPTER 23

A Sinner in an Old Farm Truck

A week later, Mark drove to the park in his used Toyota Corolla Hybrid. He and his wife had picked it out together. Between the great gas mileage and affordable price they were able to buy it outright when they sold his other car. It was hard to part with his other car, but eliminating that debt was already reaping rewards.

Mark pulled into the familiar parking lot. This wasn't a visit born of crisis or desperation. It was a visit of gratitude. The office was a different place. The fear of the takeover was gone, replaced by a buzzing, focused energy under his new leadership. At home, things were still fragile with Jen, but they were talking again, the silence replaced by a tentative, hopeful dialogue. He had even spent an entire afternoon looking through Colton's sketchbook, asking questions about the worlds his son had created, and had seen a light in his son's eyes he hadn't seen in years.

A Sinner in an Old Farm Truck

He found Silas on the bench, holding the finished wooden king in his hand. The setting sun cast long shadows across the grass.

"Silas," Mark said, sitting down. "I came to say thank you. You've… you've changed everything for me."

Silas looked up, his eyes crinkling at the corners. He held up the king. "This is just a piece of wood, Mark. The shape was already inside it. All I did was carve away the parts that weren't a king. You did the same. The leader you are now was in there all along. You just had to carve away the worry and the fear."

"I couldn't have done it without you," Mark insisted. "You've given me so much wisdom."

Silas let out a hearty laugh, a sound that surprised Mark with its volume. "Wisdom? Mark, don't put me on a pedestal. I'm just an old man with a lot of stories. And half of what people call wisdom is just the scars from their own foolishness."

He leaned back, a mischievous twinkle in his eye. "Let me tell you a story that's got nothing to do with business. A few years back, I'd just gotten new tires on my old farm truck and wanted to see how they rode. It was a beautiful day, not much traffic. Of course, a small car with a tiny engine but gigantic, buzzing tailpipes pulls up next to me. The young fella driving fits the profile—tattoos, and a hat that might as well have been embroidered with 'I'm too stupid to put this on straight.' He gives me that look, you know the one. 'Take this, grandpa.'"

Mark couldn't help but smile.

"Well," Silas continued, a grin spreading across his face, "I know judging is a sin, but a few more were about to follow. See, my truck looks like it's twenty years old, all rust and dents. But underneath, it's got a big-block engine and a high-performance transmission. It's got the heart of a sports car. So when this kid floors it, I wait till he's a couple of car lengths ahead, and then I put my accelerator to the floor. Mark, that old truck roared. I glanced in my rearview mirror, and his little car was getting smaller and smaller and smaller! When I finally looked at my speedometer, the needle was buried past one hundred. I was astonished at my own speed and, frankly, my own stupidity."

He shook his head, still chuckling. "I learned something that day. I learned that a professing man of faith, religious to the core, can become a profound sinner in the span of a single heartbeat."

Mark laughed. "So, how did those new tires test out?"

"Wonderful!" Silas's body shook as he chuckled, and they both laughed as the sun dipped below the horizon.

The story was a gift. It was Silas showing Mark that he was just a man, full of the same pride and foolishness as anyone else.

His expression grew more serious. "Wisdom doesn't always come from the foolish things, though. Sometimes it comes from the hard things." He paused, his gaze distant. "Years ago, when I was working my way up at a company, they built a big lake. A few years later, they discovered they'd inadvertently flooded a family's burial plot. The whole place was in an uproar. 'Do we drain the lake? Do we hire divers? Do we just keep quiet?' One of the engineers insisted they had to be honest. So, they found a grandson of the woman who was buried there and sent the engineer to deliver the news."

"What happened?" Mark asked, captivated.

"The engineer went to the grandson's house, sat him down, and explained with a heavy heart that his grandmother's grave was now at the bottom of their lake. And the grandson started to laugh. He said, 'Grandma was a fisherman. I can think of no happier place for her to be.' Honesty is the best policy, Mark, even when you're terrified of the outcome. It's the only way to build a foundation on solid rock instead of sand."

Silas turned to him, his expression now deeply earnest. He placed the finished wooden king in Mark's hand. It was smooth and perfect.

"You've done good work, Mark. At the office and at home. You just need to remember to treasure and nurture the good people you have around you. They are the real key to your success and happiness."

He stood up slowly, his joints creaking. From his pocket, he pulled another piece of wood. It was a pawn, identical to the one that had started Mark's journey months ago. He held it out.

Mark looked from the king in his own hand to the pawn in Silas's. "Thank you, Silas, but I don't need it. With the king, my set is complete."

A slow smile spread across Silas's face. "This isn't for you." He reached into his coat and produced a small, crisp envelope. "This is for the next person who finds themselves lost in a storm."

The image hit Mark with the force of a memory unlocked: the heavy little pawn sitting on his desk, the tiny, folded note tucked beneath it. The beginning of everything. His heart hammered in his chest.

"Silas," Mark asked, his voice barely a whisper. "That first gift… the one on my desk. Who…?"

Silas's smile didn't waver. He simply looked at Mark, his eyes full of a deep and unspoken understanding. He placed the new Pawn and the envelope on the bench beside him.

"But the most important thing I can tell you is this," he said, his voice low and full of a profound gravity. "This life is your only opportunity, for all eternity, to live by faith in Jesus. No matter what comes after, it will all be certain knowledge. This right here, this is the only time you get to trust Him without seeing. It's a gift. Don't waste it."

With that, he gave Mark a final, knowing look, turned, and began to walk away, his figure shrinking as he followed the path around the pond. Mark sat there, the wooden king in his hand, a feeling of immense gratitude mixing with a strange and sudden sense of loss, as if he had just received his final lesson.

CHAPTER 24

Pass It On

It was over a month later and all the staff were in their large meeting room, a buzz of excitement rippling through the conversations. "Tomorrow is a holiday weekend and I want to give you all a chance to start it early," Mark announced. There was clapping in the room and Mark continued, "I have made a list of things we need to get done before we leave today and whenever we finish them we can all go home. Now, the list is long and it's more than we usually get done in a day, but if we work together I think we can double our productivity. Just remember, a regular steady pace will usually outperform a stop-and-go system."

Sarah called out in the crowd, "I don't know, Mark, I am a pretty good sprinter!" The group chuckled.

Everyone looked back at Mark when he responded to Sarah, "Yeah, I know!" Mark smiled, "Last time you shot past me in traffic, I passed you when you got stuck at the next stoplight." Everyone laughed. Mark continued, "Steady beats stop-and-go. Now go make it happen." With some cheers they dispersed, accepting Mark's challenge to steadily work together.

Mark made his way back to his office and sat down. The beautiful pawn was still sitting on his desk and Mark stared at its clean, round edges. He longed to open the envelope, but it was sealed. He had been back to the park several times, but Silas was never there. Sometimes he even wondered if Silas was a real person, but knowing how much his life had changed was real enough. He just knew the envelope had to have Silas's new carving location.

Mark had thought much about who might benefit from connecting with Silas. He only had one pawn to pass on, and so he didn't want to waste it. For a while, he had considered giving it to David, but he wasn't interested in listening to anyone. Just last week, the veil seemed to get pulled from Richard's eyes, and David was no longer working there. After all the progress they had made in the last month implementing Mark's marketing ideas, their company had a new steady stream of income flowing in. Richard had not been able to envision things from a prototype or drawing with regard to marketing, but now with reality in front of him, David's fluff was evident and he was gone.

David was their second marketing director in the last year, and when Richard let him go, he told Mark, "In management situations, sometimes you must change your people. If this doesn't work, you must change your people." Then he gave the responsibility to Mark to hire a new marketing director. Right at that time, someone with a great resume had come in and asked him, "You're not hiring, are you?" Mark just shook his head, no. He knew that when someone asks a question in the negative, they are either consciously or subconsciously wanting the answer to be NO. He knew they did not want to work with them but for some reason felt the need to ask. However, Mark already knew who would be perfect. Chloe and her team had taken Mark's principles and made them happen. Under her leadership, the marketing department was thriving.

"Hey, I was talking with Clark about how we could upgrade our backend and we have got a plan that could save us a bunch of money." Mark snapped back to reality as he turned to see Kevin Tanaka poking his head in the door of his office.

Mark responded, "Give me about ten minutes, and I want to hear all about it." Kevin ducked back out and darted down the hallway. Mark smiled to himself. He had planned on firing Kevin after the massive server failure they had experienced, but it really had become a major turning point for Kevin. Once Kevin had seen his elegant masterpiece go up in flames, it humbled him and he realized that working with others was better than working in a silo. Mark had concluded, sometimes expensive mistakes are the perfect training which can make your employee worth holding onto. Kevin really was a genius at engineering; he just lacked the experience to refine his ideas in the real world. Now working with his veteran crew, they were knocking it out of the park. Mark laughed out loud as he recalled Kevin commenting on how old everyone else was on his team. Mark had told him that everyone's definition of old is your age, plus ten or fifteen years.

"What are you laughing about in here?" Jack said as he mopped the entrance to Mark's open door.

Mark chuckled, his inner humor was now exposed. "It's Kevin, before he couldn't listen to anyone else and now he is eager to get advice from anyone who would invest in him." Mark smiled as he watched Jack create a glowing reflection around him on the wet floor.

"Maybe he might appreciate that pawn that you haven't given away yet," Jack said casually as he made the last pass with the mop and then continued down the hallway. Mark turned to look at the pawn and then back to Jack. Had it been Jack who had given him the pawn in the beginning?

"Jack," Mark called out, "Do you know Silas or where he is now?"

Mark heard Jack call back down the hall, "Wisdom lives within everyone who heeds it." Mark laughed again, Jack was just as mysterious as Silas. He looked at the pawn standing there, ready to find its new owner. Jack was right, Kevin would be perfect.

It wasn't even lunchtime when everyone had finished what was on Mark's list. His little experiment had paid off. When they got back from vacation they would need to explore how they got so much more done together.

As Mark headed out of the parking lot, he passed Kevin's car. He smiled as he saw Kevin hold the pawn and note in one hand by the window. With his other hand, he was punching in an address to his GPS while glancing back and forth from the note. Mark went to his usual parking spot and sat down in his car with a deep sense of satisfaction. He was still grinning as he watched Kevin's car pull out of the lot. "Let the adventure begin," he thought to himself.

CHAPTER 25

Home

Three months later, a fierce autumn storm raged outside, the wind howling and rattling the windows of Mark's house. Not long ago, a storm like this would have mirrored the chaos in his own mind. Tonight, it was just weather. Inside, the house was an island of warmth and calm. The scent of Jen's chili simmered in the kitchen, and the soft scratch of colored pencils on paper was the only sound in the living room.

Mark sat on the floor, cross-legged, watching his son work. They were surrounded by a sea of poster board, markers, and printouts for Colton's big social studies project. The assignment was to create a visual timeline of a historical event. A few months ago, Mark would have managed this project like a failing department, with timelines, metrics, and a heavy dose of frustration. Tonight, he was just an assistant.

"Okay, so after the battle, the general sends a message back to the king," Colton narrated, his tongue sticking out in concentration as he drew a detailed picture of a messenger on horseback. "But he can't just say, 'We won.' He has to make it sound heroic. So he says…" Colton paused, looking at his dad. "What's a good word for a big victory, Dad?"

"How about 'glorious'?" Mark suggested.

"Yeah! A glorious victory!" Colton said, carefully lettering the words in a flowing, dramatic script.

Mark watched him, a sense of awe washing over him. Colton wasn't just drawing pictures; he was telling a story. He was thinking about motivation, about character, about how to convey emotion through words and images. The project wasn't a series of dates and facts to him; it was a drama. Mark, the logical engineer, could never see the world this way. He could organize facts, but he could never make them sing.

In that moment, another of Silas's truths landed in his heart, not as a lesson learned, but as a simple, observable fact. Every person is superior to you in some manner. He was the boss at work, the man with the important title. But here, on this floor, his son was the master. Colton had a gift, a way of seeing and creating that Mark could only admire. His job wasn't to fix his son's weakness in math, but to champion his incredible strength in art and storytelling.

"That looks amazing, Colton," Mark said, his voice thick with a pride that was deep and true. "You're a great artist."

Colton beamed. "Thanks, Dad."

Later, after Colton was asleep, Mark stood with Jen by the large living room window, watching the rain lash against the glass. She leaned her head on his shoulder, and he wrapped his arm around her. The tension that had lived between them for years was gone, replaced by a comfortable, easy silence.

"He's a different kid with you now," Jen said softly. "You're… present. It's all I ever wanted."

"I'm sorry it took me so long to get home," Mark said, kissing the top of her head.

"You're here now," she whispered. "That's all that matters."

They both sat down. On the table between them sat a full, intricately carved chess set. Thirty-two pieces, half of dark wood and half of light, stood facing each other ready for a game. The fireplace crackled with the family picture staring at them over its mantle. As Mark looked over the chess set, he could see all the pieces of wisdom that Silas had given him. The board was a monument to their many discussions. In the beginning, when he wondered what the meaning of the pawns were, Silas had told him it would all come together in the end. Now it had and he picked up a pawn to move it on the board. Occasionally, he went back to the park and watched the ducks. He even found a shortcut there from his work, but Silas was never there. He had a feeling he would never see the old man again, but he had thought about following Kevin on more than one occasion. Nevertheless, it didn't matter. The wisdom wasn't in the man; it was in the living.

They sat there for a long time, moving their pieces and watching the storm rage. The wind howled, but the house was steady. The rain beat down, but they were warm and dry. Mark knew there would be other storms—at work, at home, and in the world. There would always be storms.

But for the first time in his life, he wasn't afraid because Silas had helped him find the strategy to navigate his storms.

APPENDIX

Harold's "Thin Book"

The following is the "Thin Book" that Harold gave to Peter in the introduction of this book. Harold and Peter wanted to share this with you, so that you can see where the wisdom came from in the story and provide you with an opportunity to see if you found all the nuggets of insights while you were reading the novel.

The following lessons are based on Harold's personal and professional experiences over several decades. To protect the privacy of individuals, some names and identifying details have been changed.

Harold's Leadership Notes

The smartest person I ever knew was Samuel Thomas Echols, Jr. Sam had a tenth-grade education! I have worked with PhDs and many others that were brilliant people all my life. Sam outdid them all in common sense and practical application of knowledge in both living and working.

Harold's "Thin Book"

He gave me many pointers in the years we worked closely together. Not all the following came from Sam. Other people have brightened my life and given me tidbits of wisdom. Others I picked up myself after making mistakes- and learning from them.

I'm sure that unknown others added to the mixture of the various people gaining these bits of wisdom. I have heard sermons all my life. Hopefully some of them soaked in and formed some basis of my actions over the years. My kids grew up hearing these and I hope others may benefit from them.

1. MAKE EVERY BUSINESS SURPRISE A GOOD ONE. Every business transaction has the potential for surprises. Deliveries, prices or quality may vary from the expected. Make the customer happy with the outcome by allowing for any change (surprise) that may happen. In other words, under promise but over perform. (Sam)

2. PEOPLE TEND TO CONCENTRATE ON THE SMALLER OF TWO PROBLEMS. This is a good method of diversion should you need it. If you have a serious matter that causes contention (e.g. An upheaval in senior management) you can hint there may be a "departmental restructuring". Those persons will concentrate on that while your company digests the major problem and overcomes it. Also, they may come up with some good ideas on how to do a restructuring! (Sam)

3. THE ANSWER TO EVERY PROBLEM LIES IN A PROPERLY CRAFTED QUESTION. Clearly define the problem in asking the question. If you form the question correctly you are very near the answer. (Sam and also a UMR professor)

4. IF YOU CAN'T DESCRIBE SOMETHING USING NUMBERS, YOU DON'T KNOW WHAT YOU ARE TALKING ABOUT. (a UMR professor)

5. WHATEVER YOU WANT MOST IN LIFE, YOU WILL NEVER ATTAIN TO YOUR SATISFACTION. People who clamor for fame or money will never be rich or famous enough. On the other hand, if your spouse's love is your keenest desire you will make every effort to honor her and this will have a very good result. Desiring more knowledge of God is never a bad thing. (The Bible says "where your treasure is, there will be your heart also." Luke 13:34) (Harold and, of course, the Bible)

6. EVERY PERSON WORKING FOR YOU IS SUPERIOR TO YOU IN SOME MANNER. There are some ways in which your lowest paid employee is better than you. Use these skills whenever possible. (Harold)

7. MAKE SIGNAGE AND STATEMENTS POSITIVE. A retail business decided to double the factory warranty on goods purchased at that store. Somehow, they made the sign announcing this new program sound negative. This also applies to our statements and questions. Checkout clerks often ask "Is that all?". Rather ask "Would there be anything else?" This is a more positive question and may prompt the customer's memory. (Harold)

8. MAKE YOUR SIGNS AND LOGOS READABLE. Too often companies make their signage so fancy with script, etc. they cannot be read without effort. Think of the person that does not already know what your sign says. (Harold)

9. THE LORD GAVE YOU TWO EARS AND ONE MOUTH. USE THEM IN THAT PERSPECTIVE. LISTEN TO PEOPLE. You learn when you listen, not when you talk. I once got a phone call from a man I did not know. He asked if we could make some

10 oz. cup dispensers for him. At that time 4, 6 and 8-ounce cup dispensers were the industry standard and no one made bigger ones-including our factory. I told him that I would check our tooling to see if it could be expanded to allow for the bigger diameter needed and would call him back. I then walked out to the shop to see what would be required and found that only a few simple modifications would be needed. I got an order for samples with that return call and a massive order when he liked the samples. Rudy became a great customer and a good phone buddy over the next years. He later told me that he had called nearly every manufacturer of this type of item and was routinely turned down-often rudely. Listening to him really paid off. When 10 oz. dispensers later became an item of demand, we were already tooled up for production. (Sam & Rudy Orisec)

10. SILENCE IS GOLDEN-AND A POWERFUL TOOL. People are often uncomfortable when a conversation becomes quiet. They tend to want to fill the void with information-anything. A very dear friend, that is an HR rep, uses this tool in her interviews with prospective employees. At some point she will sit quietly and not say anything. Very often they will start talking-often saying things they would rather you not know just to fill the void. She learns much about the person in this manner. I used this recently. Walking into an antique shop, I told the owner I was considering an item on display outside. He said that it was marked $195. I remained expressionless and QUIET. He then gave me a reduced price. Without my uttering a word, my cost went down. (Harold & Shanna Sloan)

11. LIVE BELOW YOUR MEANS. Being in control of your finances is a wonderful way of relieving stress in your life. Devoting your life to GOD and being completely faithful to your spouse are even more important. (Harold and Dave Ramsey) A financially successful friend once told me that DEBT is a four-letter word. (John Anhang)

12. IF PRESSURED FOR A QUICK ANSWER, ALWAYS SAY "NO". (Sam)

13. BEING CONCERNED ABOUT SOMETHING IS OK. BEING WORRIED ABOUT IT IS NOT. Concern implies your coming corrective action. Worry simply drags you down without result. (Sam)

14. NO MATTER HOW PROFOUND AND CORRECT YOU ARE ABOUT SOMETHING, THERE WILL BE DETRACTORS. Do not allow them to drag you down and do not respond to them. They are usually not profound thinkers and you will not alter their opinion. (Harold)

15. YOU CAN'T SLING MUD WITHOUT GETTING DIRTY. (Harold)

16. DON'T HOLD MEETINGS IN YOUR OFFICE. You cannot control the time structure in this manner. If you call a meeting in the conference room, however, you are free to leave should the need occur. (Harold)

17. IF YOU WRONG SOMEONE IN PRIVATE THE APOLOGY SHOULD BE MADE IN PRIVATE. IF YOU HARM SOMEONE IN PUBLIC, THE CORRECTION MUST BE MADE PUBLICLY. (Sam)

18. WHEN CONGRATULATING SOMEONE DO IT PUBLICLY. IF CHEWING THEM OUT DO IT IN PRIVATE. Never discipline someone in front of others. Think about the emotions and lasting effects of this. When bragging about someone in front of others, those other people will be thinking about what they need to do in order to excel. If disciplining someone in front of others, everyone in the room will do everything possible to make sure that doesn't happen to them-including not taking a risk to find a better way to do their job! (Sam)

19. BE CAREFUL IN DEFINING YOUR BUSINESS OR PURPOSE. Charter Carburetor thought they built carburetors. If they had realized that they built "fuel delivery systems to engines", they might now be building fuel injectors- and still be in business! (Harold)

20. NO ONE KNOWS THE JOB BETTER THAN THE PERSON DOING IT. If you are thinking of a change in a process, talk to the person doing that job early on. That person may say "that won't work BECAUSE.........." and you might have saved lots of time and dollars with your new knowledge. However, that person may say something like "that would work IF......." and you now have a new perspective of the idea AND a new ally in getting the job done. Afterall, it is also now HIS idea! (Sam) This also applies to someone on the job coming to you with an idea. Pay attention. There may be an important aspect in that idea that you had not considered as an issue or problem. Remember, that person knows it best. Respect the courage it took to come to you. (Harold)

21. DELEGATE WHEN YOU CAN. You cannot personally handle every detail and others will grow and mature in the process. (Sam)

22. WHEN YOU PUT A SUBORDINATE IN A POSITION REQUIRING HIM TO MAKE A DECISION, GO WITH THAT DECISION. You may wish to discuss that decision later with him privately. If at all possible, go with his action for now. (Sam)

23. WHEN SOMEONE IS SMILING AS THEY SAY "I'M SORRY" OR IF THEY USE A CATCH PHRASE LIKE "SORRY ABOUT THAT", THEY ARE NOT SORRY. (Harold)

24. YOU ONLY WIN AT THINGS YOU FOCUS ON. (Harold)

25. IF THE PERSON OVERSEEING A PROJECT IS NOT ON BOARD WITH IT, THE PROJECT HAS A LOW CHANCE OF SUCCESS. (Harold)

26. ANYTIME SOMEONE USES A PHRASE SUCH AS "I'M TELLING YOU THE TRUTH" OR "I'M NOT LYING ABOUT THIS", DISTRUST HIM. Why would an honest person ever say those things? (Harold)

27. YOU NEED PEOPLE AROUND YOU THAT WILL VOICE THEIR TRUE OPINION. Yes-men can get you in trouble and possibly lead you down a wrong path. You can acquire these better people by being approachable to ALL your employees on a regular basis. (Harold)

28. MAKE HASTE SLOWLY. I first heard this from Sam, but later heard it attributed to Abraham Lincoln.

29. WHEN AWARDING OR PRAISING AN EMPLOYEE, MAKE SURE THE SPOUSE AND FAMILY SEE IT TOO. (Harold)

30. PLANT THE SEED OF AN IDEA IN OTHERS AND WATCH IT GROW. A project has a better chance of success when the person(s) doing it were involved with the idea. Nurture the seed (idea) as needed. (Harold)

31. IT AIN'T A SALE UNTIL THE MONEY FLOWS. After signing a purchase contract on a farm, I immediately began clearing brush on it-before we closed on the property. Bob Grisham, a Real Estate agent, kindly pointed out that the property was not yet mine and repercussions could result. This parallels the old saying of "not counting your chickens before they hatch". (Bob)

32. PAY YOUR SUPPLIERS AS QUICKLY AS YOU POSSIBLY CAN. You depend on them for your product and this practice will build unbelievable appreciation from them. They will make every effort to work with you and to keep your business. We had a rubber stamp that said "This invoice was paid on the day it was received. Date _____". Our suppliers liked that and showed it with their improved service. I asked Tom Depew, the man that first told me of this practice, about shorted shipments or defective goods. His answer-"if you don't trust them, don't do business with them. Honest suppliers will make the needed corrections". The advantages of this practice will be far better than any interest earned by paying your bills on the last day available to you. I was also on the receiving end of this practice by one of my dealers. Jerrod Larado would send in a nice order (everything was done by snail-mail in those days) and enclose a blank signed check. The line for the written amount would say something like "not to exceed ten thousand dollars". I thoroughly enjoyed that and told him so. And, yes, Jerrod 's shipments were always the first to go out no matter how much backlog we had. (Tom DePew and Jerrod Larado)

33. WHEN WORKING WITH A BUDGET DO NOT ADOPT THE "USE IT OR LOSE IT" CONCEPT. Rather return any unspent funds to the company's coffers for use where needed. In the long term your budget requests will be better received and the money will be better used for the business. (Shanna Sloan)

34. MANY PEOPLE CANNOT ENVISION FROM A PROTOTYPE OR DRAWINGS. (Harold)

35. DON'T WORK SO HARD THAT YOU FORGET TO MANAGE. You can save a few dollars in one spot while lots of money is being lost elsewhere due to your lack of attention. Keep your eye on the big picture. I once noticed a production line was falling behind and jumped in to help. Sam walked by and said that while I was working here, the guys in back were having a party. They weren't, but his point was well taken. (Sam)

36. THE WORKER ALWAYS GOES FIRST. When you encounter one of your employees in a doorway or other narrow space, always give them the right-of-way. When doing so, I comment that "the worker always goes first". This is a simple, yet effective, way to show your respect and to acknowledge their importance to the business. (Harold)

37. YOUR EMPLOYEES WILL FOCUS ON WHAT THEY BELIEVE IS IMPORTANT TO YOU. If you walk past a piece of paper on the floor they may do so also. Picking up that bit of trash will let them know of your dislike of that situation and they will correct their habits. You don't have to go around cleaning the building but communicate by word or action your priorities. (Brian Briley)

38. IN AN EMERGENCY SITUATION, TAKE A MENTAL STEP BACK AND AWAY. Look around at what is being done and what is NOT being taken care of. Do not get distracted with lesser things during critical events. (Harold)

39. WHEN YOU NEED TO MAKE A DECISION-MAKE IT. Consider the obvious pros and cons and then make your move. Do not vacillate back and forth wondering about your choice. Only if you see an obvious and serious error, or if conditions vary, should you change directions. Trust both your gut and experience in the matter. (Harold)

40. A PERSON THAT WILL STEAL FOR YOU, WILL STEAL FROM YOU. A friend with a retail business caught a clerk intentionally short-changing a customer. He fired him immediately even though the clerk protested that the amount gained was for the boss. The owner knew that a thief is a thief and their moral code is not restrictive. They will eventually steal from anyone, even friends and family. Do not tolerate a thief in any manner. This also applies to a person that will lie. (Harold and Shanna Sloan)

41. A machine OPERATOR is so adept and attuned to his machine that he merely has to THINK of what needs to be done and the machine seems to react to it. Anything less and the person on the machine is only a DRIVER. (Harold)

42. EFFECTIVE LEADERS SHARE THE CREDIT BUT SHOULDER THE BLAME. When a project succeeds, be sure everyone involved gets noticed. If it fails, man-up. (Harold)

43. A CON MAN LIVES ON THE EDGE OF LEGALITY. (Harold)

44. CONSIDER EVERY SITUATION A LEARNING EXPERIENCE. (Harold)

45. Whether you think you can or think you cannot, you are correct. (Henry Ford)

46. FOCUS ON YOUR LONGTIME GOALS. Drive the business, and your life, in that direction. (Harold)

47. AS A LEADER, IT IS YOUR DUTY TO HELP YOUR PEOPLE IMPROVE THEMSELVES. This can mean encouraging them to further their formal education even when you suspect they will move on with that degree. It also can mean writing a good recommendation for them when you do not want them to leave. Holding them back is a disservice. (Harold and Shanna Sloan)

48. A REGULAR STEADY PACE WILL USUALLY OUTPERFORM A STOP-AND-GO SYSTEM. A person with a steady pace will outproduce another person that works faster but takes more breaks. Did you ever notice that the guy that shot past you in traffic is now sitting beside you at the next stop light? (Harold)

49. When arriving at a destination, back into the parking spot if possible. You are a more alert driver upon arrival than you will be when leaving. Your thoughts when leaving may be on your meeting or destination and not as much on driving. This is the safer method. Also, when possible, park next to some barricade. Other cars can only damage yours on one side in that event-you are 50% safer. (Harold & Shanna Sloan)

50. When purchasing materials consumed on a regular basis (e.g. nuts and bolts) in which you have a standard or specifications to go by, shop for price and delivery. Save every penny as long as the service is appropriate. However, when buying tools or other long-term items, go for quality. Price is not as significant in this situation and you will long enjoy the improvements. (Sam)

51. THE PROPER RESPONSE TO "THANK YOU" IS "YOU ARE WELCOME". "No problem" is NOT the proper way to respond. (Harold)

52. "SORRY ABOUT YOUR WAIT" sounds like "SORRY ABOUT YOUR WEIGHT". "I APPOLOGIZE FOR THE DELAY" is better. (Harold)

53. LEAD rather than DRIVE your employees. I have known a manager that threatened his employees in order to get their jobs done. They hated the job and him. His eventual replacement has made all the difference in the business atmosphere and the public can see it. The workers are smiling now when customers walk in. (Harold)

54. SOME BUSINESSES GO ALL OUT TO ATTRACT NEW CUSTOMERS BUT NEGLECT THEIR EXISTING ONES. Spend time and effort to keep those that are already walking through your doors. (Harold)

55. FIND FUN WAYS TO CHALLENGE YOUR EMPLOYEES. In a factory setting, the day before a holiday break is notorious for not getting much work done. Your people are mentally preoccupied with their family time and the coming days off from work. One Wednesday before Thanksgiving break, I met the people at the door as they arrived for work. I handed out a job list and told them we would all go home when the list was finished! The list contained more than a typical day's work and they knew it. However, they flew into the jobs (even before starting time) and got busy. During the day, I often had to remind them to not run in the building. Otherwise, all went well and quickly. When some of them finished their list, they jumped over to help others (such is the benefit of our cross-training efforts prior to this). By noon, all the work was finished, the shop was clean and the group of very happy and proud people met me at the door. They walked out with a full paycheck and smiles on their faces-and we all knew what could be done! (Harold)

56. PICK YOUR BATTLES AND TIME THEM. There are times when conditions will not allow success for your next project. Spend time rearranging those situations before starting the war. (Harold)

57. AVOID SPIT AND POLISH REGIMENS. Your battles will not occur in straight lines. (Moshe Dayan)

58. IN A RETAIL SITUATION, STREAMLINE CHECK-OUT TIME. A local business has their check-out people answering incoming phone calls and handling returns. Those items get priority over the customers waiting in line and often add a considerable amount of time the paying customer must wait. I have seen people put down their intended purchases and walk out. This store's effort to save a few dollars by multi-tasking actually costs them. If you find abandoned items around your cash registers you might want to question why. (Harold)

59. DON'T GIVE SPEECHES, RATHER TELL STORIES. A speech is a three-point discussion given after a rubber-chicken banquet. Even the best speakers can only be remembered for a short time. However, a well told story can be remembered for decades. Just make it fit your topic. (Harold)

60. IT IS OK TO TEST YOUR PEOPLE BUT LOOK MORE FOR STRENGTHS THAN WEAKNESSES. You will find weaknesses but look further for their good points. When I first started working at the factory as a very young man, I performed various tasks to learn the business. One day I was packing machines when I noticed a casting laying on the packing bench. On that particular machine, we removed a 4 lb. casting before packing and then wrapped the casting and placed it inside the box separately. I had apparently missed putting the casting in one of the boxes. I reflected for a moment and then started weighing each box to determine the one missing a casting. Sam was standing nearby and said, "you don't have to do that." I responded that I had left a casting out of a box and he then told me that he had actually put an extra casting on the bench to see how I would react. My decision to weigh the boxes really impressed him as no one had thought of that before. Others started opening boxes. I'm guessing that a few had ignored the possible problem and thus did not enjoy long-term employment with the company. My better method of handling the situation went a long way in our relationship and I eventually bought that business from him upon his retirement. I passed his test! (Sam & Harold)

61. SELL THAT LAST CIGAR. Many years ago, a small-town tobacco shop owner would not sell the last cigar in any box. She didn't want to run out of stock! It didn't make sense then-and doesn't now. (Harold)

62. Definition of OLD AGE. Your current age plus 10 or 15 years. (Harold)

63. YOU'RE NOT HIRING ARE YOU? When someone asks a question in the negative, they are either consciously or subconsciously wanting the answer to be NO. This person does not want to work for you but for some reason feels the need to ask. Save both of you some grief and kindly send him away. (Harold)

64. THINK ABOUT THOSE CATCH PHRASES OFTEN USED. Gene and Ruth Darr were an elderly couple in a small town where I once lived. They were wonderful people and sincerely loved all children but had not been blessed with their own. One day Gene asked about my small kids and I said "growing like weeds!" He instantly corrected me. "No, they are growing like FLOWERS!" In that one simple statement, Gene profoundly altered my perception of my own children and those around me for all time. In that vein, I no longer tell kids they are "getting big". I say they are "getting tall!" They like that more. Frankly, I am a little bothered by "Have a good one" or someone I've never seen before calling me "Honey", "sweetie" or "Dear". Sir or Ma'am are better. (Gene Darr and Harold)

65. An employee can have 20 years of experience---or one year's experience 20 times. (Sam)

66. THIS LIFE IS YOUR ONLY OPPORTUNITY, FOR ALL ETERNITY, TO LIVE BY FAITH. No matter where you spend eternity after your time here, everything there will be certain knowledge. Faith is a blessing that can only be treasured now. (Harold)

67. TREASURE AND NURTURE THE GOOD PEOPLE YOU HAVE AROUND YOU-IN BOTH BUSINESS AND LIFE. They are a key to your success and happiness. (Harold)

68. Your life should be based on truth, but two people that you should NEVER lie to are your doctor and your lawyer. (Sam)

69. CHERISH THE HARD TIMES. Mature couples tend to smile and hold hands when discussing those difficult situations they endured together. They never seem to remember the times when money was available or the kids were all healthy. However, those episodes they conquered together drew them closer. (Harold)

70. "If you play the other man's game, you will always lose." Don't work like your competition does. Play by your own rules. (Allen Benton)

71. THERE ARE SOME PERSONS WHOSE SENSE OF HUMOR MUST HAVE BEEN SURGICALLY REMOVED AT BIRTH. You cannot infuse a humor medication into them. They will die and never have laughed. Be careful where you place them in your business. In a restaurant that displayed signs saying "kids eat free all weekend", I asked the waitress what was the earliest time I could drop them off the next Saturday morning. I thought that was funny. She did not. I sat through her lecture about child neglect. In another restaurant at another time, I ordered "iced tea-without onion". The waitress was smiling as she walked away. When she delivered my tea, she also brought a small dish of sliced onions, "on the side". We all laughed and she got a nice tip! (Harold)

72. A man that will tell you where he catches fish or finds mushrooms will lie about other things too. (Harold)

73. Before illegal drugs were a problem, rural murders were usually over a woman or a dog. (Bob Grisham)

74. Beware of the SHAKEN SACK. Often someone reporting to you will have an issue with that person's employees he or she cannot resolve. They will then bring the problem up the chain-of-command to you. Picture those problems as a sack full of skunks. Your subordinate may have given that bag a good shake just before handing it to you. Those skunks inside the bag are now ready to spray their odors on whomever opens the bag! Be ready and prepared when you venture into this issue. (Sam Echols)

75. A local building inspector was gruff with the builders when examining their work. He talked down to them and otherwise failed to gain their respect. In effect, he was working AGAINST them rather than WITH them. (Harold)

76. Never argue with a reporter. They start every day with an empty newspaper and must fill it with something. You may not fare well. (Sam Echols)

77. IT PAYS TO GET ALONG WITH YOUR NEIGHBORS. A grouchy man lived next to a prissy lady. Every morning, the man would let his dog out to "do his business" and wait at his door for the dog's return. The dog would make a run for the neighbor lady's landscaping and made his deposit. The lady spoke to her neighbor about this and asked that he take the dog out on a leash to control the locations of the dog droppings. The neighbor was gruff with her and refused. The lady said nothing more. The next spring when the man went out to fire up his grill for the season's first barbeque, he opened the lid of the grill to find a winter's supply of dog droppings piled neatly inside. (Harold)

78. THE MOST DANGEROUS THING IN THE WORLD IS A BRAND-NEW ENGINEERING DEGREE. (a UMR professor)

79. There is only one time in which you don't need a strong national defense. This is when you have one. Everybody is your friend when you are strong. (Harold)

80. Rethink your approach to a problem if the answer does not happen as you wish. I was once remodeling a rental apartment and decided to replace the refrigerator. The old one was working but the new kitchen needed an updated model. I took the old unit out to the sidewalk and put a "FREE" sign on it. It stayed there for several days. I finally took the "FREE" sign away and replaced it with a "$10" sign. It was stolen that night! (Harold)

81. Don't name something in honor of someone that is still alive. They can still embarrass you. (Sam)

82. Typical GOVERNMENT specifications: Measure it with a micrometer, mark it with a piece of chalk, and cut it with an axe. (Harold)

83. In management situations you sometimes must change your people. If this doesn't work, you must change your people. (Jim Sucharski)

84. The trouble with people that don't know what they are talking about is they don't know when to stop. (Tom Smothers)

85. Women want LOVE, while men want RESPECT. (Harold)

86. Too often people confuse Government with Common sense. (Harold)

87. Younger employees only look at the money from their jobs. Retirement and insurance will not impress them. Middle aged and older workers consider these things. (Harold)

88. People do not like change. This is a factor in every update you consider. (Harold)

89. Girls tend to marry like their Dad. If their father is a good provider, faithful to his wife and family, shows love at every opportunity and disciplines with love this is the "norm" to his daughters. Any young man showing tendencies otherwise will not get a second date. (Harold)

90. By the third paycheck after a payraise, your people will have forgotten the old pay amount and the raise. The new amount on the check is now the norm. (Harold)

91. We are quick to tell an employee when we see something being done wrong, but it is also a good thing to comment when you see something being done well. Positive reinforcement goes a long way and will be remembered. (Harold)

92. When you cannot get the lid off that new jar of pickles, try tightening it. You won't feel it move but it will probably loosen at the next effort. (Harold)

93. If you have developed a new item and competition is not a factor, price the item accordingly. The price conveys the perceived value of the item. (Harold)

94. When your crew is fully capable, just tell them what you want done and turn them loose. If you were hiring a master painter for a portrait, you wouldn't tell him HOW to paint, just WHAT to paint.

95. Lastly, do not solve all the problems in your business. Rather, save a couple of small ones. If your employees do not have something to complain about, they may invent a large problem. (Harold)

Here are a few additional items of interest.

A. FIND SUBTLE WAYS TO IMPROVE YOUR BUSINESS PLAN. A friend has a lawn care service in which he has decided to do all the work himself and not hire employees. He constantly gets requests from potential customers but has no additional time with which to serve them. He purges his customer list each year by about 10% of the customers that he least prefers. Maybe these people are hard to satisfy, slow to pay or their lawns are more difficult to mow. He will then take on additional customers to replace those he has politely notified he can no longer serve. His customer list (and income) is constantly improving and he enjoys his work even more.

B. HONESTY IS THE BEST POLICY. I worked my way through college by spending every-other semester in the Engineering office at Pilot Knob Pellet Company. This was their very early days of development and was a tremendous addition to my education. One day I was in the Engineering room when lots of activity started and many people were whispering. Of course, my interest was roused. A Vice President walked by with whom I had become a friend. I asked what

Harold's "Thin Book"

was going on. He told me they had just learned the company had flooded a family burial site when the company lake was built! Somehow, this information had been lost during development of the lake but was now evident. Some of the topics were, do we hide this? Do we drain the lake? Do we get divers to exhume the grave? There was no agreement on how to proceed. One of the Engineers insisted that they be truthful about it and tell the family of the now-submerged family grave. A search located a Grandson in another state. The Engineer that had insisted on being truthful was appointed to deliver the news to the family. Upon his return he was all smiles. He had gone to the home of the Grandson and sat down to tell him about the inadvertent flooding of his Grandmother's grave. The guy started laughing and then said, "Grandma was a fisherman. I can think of no happier place for her than at the bottom of your lake." Grandma's still in the lake!

C. YOUR SPECIAL SKILLS ARE VALUABLE. DO NOT DIMINISH THE PERCEPTION OF THEM. An artist friend would take a job and then work all night to complete the work and deliver it quickly. The problem was that his customers did not value his work as much since he obviously did not require much time to make the piece. He started intentionally taking more time to make, or at least to deliver, the artwork and noticed the customer's appreciation of his skills improve.

D. DRAMA CAN HELP. A regular, and unwelcome, visitor to my office would often come in to complain about something and stay long past his welcome. I don't remember him ever coming in with anything positive or helpful. One day I was especially busy. He had ranted for some time and I needed him to leave. I noticed my glasses on the desk and picked them up, twisted them into two pieces and threw them against the far office wall. I yelled, "I'VE HAD ENOUGH

OF THIS!." He promptly left my office-and never returned. On the way home that day, I stopped at a local discount store to replace those broken reading glasses-at a total cost of $1 plus tax. That was one of the best dollars I've ever spent.

E. It is usually not the major things you do for someone that is most remembered by them. People have approached me to thank me for something I did for them in years past. In nearly every case it was some minor comment or deed that I did not remember. A now well-known minister once shook my hand to thank me for something I did for him that changed his life for the better. I was thinking of some big donation or other deed in my past, but he reminded me of my encouragement to him after hearing him give his very first sermon in our community church. He told me that was what he needed to get him past his own doubts at the time.

F. HAVE FUN IN THIS LIFE. My daily-driver vehicles are a couple of old farm pickups. I once had new tires put on one of them and wanted to see how smoothly they rode. I took southbound 67 highway out of Farmington as a test drive. It was a beautiful day with very little traffic, clear road and good visibility. Of course, a small car pulled up next to me with a small engine but gigantic tail pipes. You know, those tailpipes that give off that very loud irritating buzzing noise for all to hear. This young driver looked over at me as he pulled up alongside as if to say "take this, grandpa". He fit the profile, skinny, tattoos, and wore a hat that should have been emblazoned with "I'm too stupid to put this hat on straight." (I know, judging is a sin. More sins would soon follow.) I now digress. This particular old farm truck is a 2001 3/4-ton 4-wheel drive Silverado 2500HD. Some of you by now have figured out that this truck has a big-block 8.1-liter gasoline engine with a high-performance Allison transmission. It is a VERY fast and powerful truck. Outside it shows

20 years of life complete with rust and dents, but the drivetrain has the heart of a sports car. When this kid shot the power to his tiny engine (about 1/3 the size of mine) I waited until he had pulled out by a couple of car lengths and pushed my accelerator to the floor and held it there. As my truck kept going faster and faster and faster, I glanced into my rear-view mirror to see that his car was getting smaller and smaller and smaller! When I finally looked at my speedometer (that is registered for 100 MPH and the needle was buried beyond that) I was astonished to see my speed and immediately backed off the pedal and allowed the truck to coast back to the speed limit where the cruise control again took over. I drove at the speed limit for next few miles until I arrived at my exit. That little car followed me past that exit, but never got near me again. Did he learn a lesson? I like to think he now has a new respect for geezers and a fear of geezers driving old farm trucks. Did I learn a lesson? You bet. I learned that a professing CHRISTIAN, religious to the core (probably to the point of being obnoxious about it) can become a profound sinner in the time span of one heartbeat. While I asked for forgiveness of my many sins that day, I'm not sure that the ONE TRUE GOD honored that request because I was smiling as I described those sins. I know HE was in the truck with me that day but I doubt that HE was hanging on for dear life as I should have been. To my law-enforcement friends reading this, I don't plan to ever again approach that speed in any vehicle I may drive. To those wanting to know how those new tires tested out-WONDERFUL. (Harold)

G. WHEN INSPECTING SOMEONE'S WORK FOR PROBLEMS, POINT OUT THE POSITIVE TOO. A young friend was working as an intern with a construction company. Her college major was Safety and she was traveling with a company manager to the various work sites. Her job was to enforce safety rules and she was to file a report whenever she saw something being done badly or against the safety rules. This put her in a negative position with the people. She decided to also comment whenever she saw something being done well. It has completely changed her attitude and that of those around her. Positive reinforcement is a great teacher and she enjoys her job even more. (Harold)

H. IT'S WORTH IT TO BE CHARITABLE. I give a lot of money each year to charities. Yes, much of this donation is for tax issues. I have realized that most of those people benefiting from this charitable giving do not work! On the other hand, the servers in a restaurant are working hard to see that my wishes are met and that I am happy with my meal. For that reason, I tip very well. (Harold)

These are some of the things I have learned over my decades of business and management. I hope they kick start others on their way to a successful life and career. While these items are geared toward business practices they also apply to life and your manner of living.

My best to you,

Harold Gallaher

GET A FREE COPY
Audiobook Download

If you have purchased the printed or digital edition of this book, you may download a free complementary audiobook of Proven Leadership Strategies: A Novel for Navigating Storms. To download the audiobook, please go to: ***https://togethertransformed.com/leadership-audio/***

or scan the following QR code:

After you add the audiobook to your cart, you can use the following **coupon code** to get the audiobook for free: **4LEADERS2HEAR**

To find more great titles on personal and professional development by Peter Schrock, go to:

https://TogetherTransformed.com

www.ingramcontent.com/pod-product-compliance
Lightning Source LLC
Chambersburg PA
CBHW022117040426
42450CB00006B/736